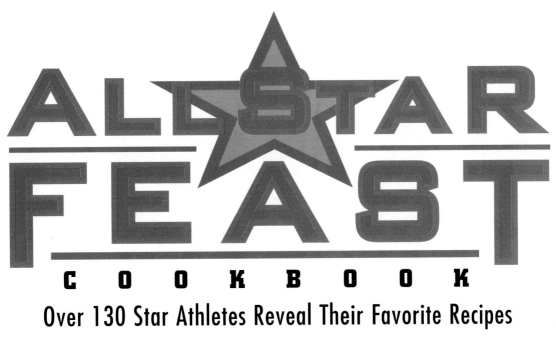

ALL STAR FEAST

COOKBOOK

Over 130 Star Athletes Reveal Their Favorite Recipes

Compiled by Wendy Diamond

Global Liaisons, Incorporated/Publishers New York

Published in 1997 by Global Liaisons, Incorporated.
P.O. Box 6049, New York, New York 10150

All Star Feast Cookbook: Over 130 Star Athletes reveal their favorite Recipes
Compiled by Wendy Diamond. — 1st edition.

This book was published as a fund raiser in support of athletics and physical fitness. Seventy percent of Global Liaisons, Incorporated's net profits will be donated to the following sports-related charities: the Buoniconti Fund to Cure Paralysis, Special Olympics International and the Women's Sports Foundation.

Most of the recipes contained in this book have been tested and edited from their original form. Some recipes have been maintained in their original form to reflect the personality of the recipe's contributor. Global Liaisons, Incorporated, all contributors, the charitable organizations and sponsors take no responsibility for any liability arising out of any injury of any kind which may be sustained from participation in or connection with the making or utilization of the recipes included in this publication.

Publisher & Art Director, Wendy Diamond
Profiles Editor, J.B. Morris, Sports Illustrated
Recipe Editor, Rita Wolfson
Sports Editor, Craig Stanton
Photo Editors, Peter Orlowsky, AllSport
            Matt Ginella, Sports Illustrated
Contributing Editors, Bob Benjamin, Elizabeth Parella, Catherine Williams
Production Director, Tom Freet, Beckley Press

ISBN 0-9647316-1-4
UPC 719340824701
Library of Congress Catalog Card Number 97-093426

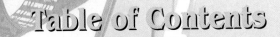

Table of Contents
Menu ...

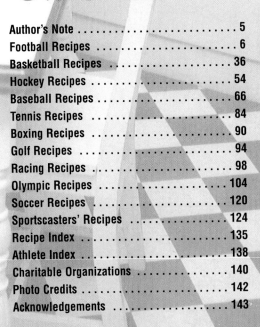

Just for the **FUN** of it. Just for the **STYLE** of it. Just for the **LOOK** of it. Just for the **FEEL** of it. Just for the **TASTE** of it.™

Diet Coke
TRADEMARK

Author's Note

When my first cookbook, A Musical Feast, featuring recipes from more than 100 musical artists including *Madonna*, *Vince Gill* and *Frank Sinatra*, raised $350,000 for the Homeless in 1995, I knew I was on to something good.

The idea for All Star Feast occurred to me when I was working on A Musical Feast. I was living in an apartment above **Mickey Mantle's** restaurant in New York City. I'd drop in time to time, and Mickey would ask when I was going to publish his "secret" recipe for the restaurant's chicken fried steak. Delicious as it is, I couldn't use it because Mickey wasn't a musician. But he got me thinking.

Now I am proud to present an All Star Feast offering favorite recipes from the kitchens of the world's best-known athletes and sports figures. Proceeds from the sale of each cookbook will be donated to the *Special Olympics International*, the *Buoniconti Fund to Cure Paralysis* and the *Women's Sports Foundation*.

As with the first book, this one came together in weird and wonderful ways, and led me into situations I never could have imagined. Like the time I was invited to appear on "Oprah" while I was promoting A Musical Feast: On the way to the studio, I found myself sharing a car with one of football's all-time greats, **Lynn Swann** of the Pittsburgh Steelers. When I was growing up in Chagrin Falls, Ohio, my dad was an avid fan of the Browns, arch rivals of the Steelers. Nevertheless by the time we arrived at the studio, I had in my hand the recipes for Lynn's delicious cornbread and his tasty Monangahela shrimp. Who knew?

Later in the green room, I found myself in the shadow of a seven foot giant. I thought maybe Oprah was doing a segment on the world's tallest man, but it turned out to be Washington Wizard's center **Juwan Howard** who was there to talk about the importance of reading. I wouldn't let him leave the green room until I had his mom's no bake chocolate oatmeal cookie recipe.

And who would have thought that attending the premiere of the movie "*Jerry Maquire*" would have resulted in recipes from two of the world's best gymnasts? I was introduced to Olympic champion **Kerri Strug's** agent Leigh Steinberg (who also represents Troy Aikman, and most of the top NFL quarterbacks) and later in the evening I happened to be standing next to another Olympic gold medalist, **Shannon Miller**, in the dessert line.

My biggest coup was when I was invited to the ESPY Awards (the ESPN Sports Awards). By the end of the evening I walked away with a seven day work out plan from **Dan O'Brien** and a healthy diet to go with it by **Amy Van Dyken**. She also contributed her apricot chicken and Dan gave his specialty, Decathalon Chicken Fajitas for the book! I also managed to cajole other Olympic gold medalists into coming up with some winning dishes, including **Michael Johnson's** protein fish dish and **Picabo Street's** mysterious morels.

It's been an exciting two year journey, and you are holding the result in your hands. For me, watching sports has become a whole other experience. Now I watch professional sports in a completely different way. I appreciate watching **Pete Sampras** return an impossible volley, or **Michael Jordan** fly through the air as he racks up points, knowing that they, and all of the athletes in my book were willing to touch the lives of people less fortunate by contributing recipes and photos to an All Star Feast.

Eat well, be happy!

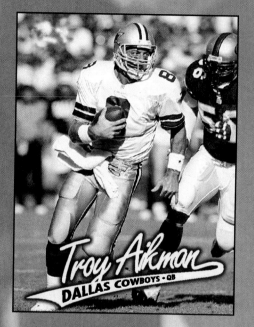

Troy Aikman
DALLAS COWBOYS · QB

Chicken Breasts Alfredo

This dish is an Oklahoma and Texas combination treat. Beef isn't the only food of choice in Big D — try some of this Chicken Breasts Alfredo and see for yourself.

6	boneless chicken breasts
1/2	cup flour
3	eggs, beaten
3	tablespoons water
1/2	cup grated Romano cheese
1/4	cup snipped parsley
1/2	teaspoon salt
1	cup fine bread crumbs
3	tablespoons vegetable oil
	Cheese Sauce, see recipe below
6	slices mozzarella cheese

Heat oven to 425. Coat chicken with flour. In a medium bowl, mix eggs, water, Romano cheese, parsley and salt. Dip chicken in egg mixture, then into bread crumbs. Heat butter and oil in large skillet. Cook chicken over medium heat until browned, about 15 minutes. Remove chicken to 11 x 7 baking dish. Make cheese sauce.

Pour cheese sauce over chicken. Top each piece with a slice of cheese. Bake until cheese melts and chicken is tender, about 8 minutes.

Serves 6.

CHEESE SAUCE

1	cup heavy cream
1/4	cup water
1/4	butter
1/2	cup grated Romano cheese
1/4	cup chopped parsley

Heat cream, water and butter in 1 quart saucepan until butter melts. Add cheese, cook and stir over medium heat 5 minutes. Stir in parsley.

Aired-Out Apple Crispy

5	cups peeled, sliced tart apples
1	teaspoon cinnamon
1	teaspoon grated lemon peel
1	teaspoon grated orange peel
2	tablespoons Grand Marnier
2	tablespoons almond liqueur
3/4	cup sugar
3/4	cup flour
1/2	cup butter
1/4	cup firmly packed brown sugar
1/4	teaspoon salt
Cream, whipped cream or ice cream	

Preheat oven to 350°. Grease a 2-quart, round baking dish. Arrange apple slices in bottom of dish. Sprinkle evenly with cinnamon, peels and liqueurs. Combine sugars, flour, butter and salt in medium bowl until crumbly. Sprinkle over apples. Bake until golden, about 45 to 60 minutes. Serve warm. Serves 6 to 8

Patriotic White Chicken Chili

1	pound large white beans
6	cups chicken broth
2	cloves garlic, minced
2	medium onions, chopped
2	4-ounce cans chopped green chilies
2	teaspoons ground cumin
1-1/2	teaspoons dried oregano
1/4	teaspoon ground cloves
1/4	teaspoon cayenne pepper
4	cups diced chicken breasts
3	cups grated Monterey jack cheese

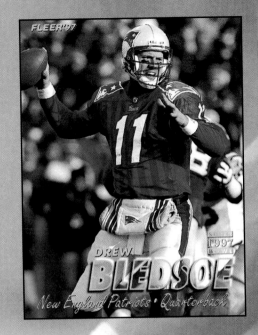

Combine beans, chicken broth, garlic and half of the onions in a large soup pot and bring to a boil. Reduce heat and simmer until beans are tender, about 3 hours. Add more broth if necessary. Saute remaining onions in oil until tender. Add chilies and seasoning and mix thoroughly. Add to bean mixture. Add chicken and continue to simmer for 1 hour.

Serve this topped with the grated cheese. It is excellent with corn bread. Serves 6 to 8.

Anderson

Sunday Morning Colorado Omelette

This is best served with banana or nut bread, bacon, and a steaming hot cup of coffee.

3	eggs beaten
1	tablespoon butter
	Salt and pepper to taste
1/2	cup shredded mozzarella cheese
1/2	cup diced tomato
2	sausage patties, cooked and crumbled into small pieces
	Diced jalapeno peppers (to taste)
1	avocado, sliced
1	large tortilla
	Salsa
	Sour Cream

Over the past 25 years I have been spending as much time as possible at my ranch on the Colorado River near Vail. Most mornings I am up early and only a wet line and a great hunger!! Therefore, I developed this delicious omelette recipe in order to keep my family and guests quiet about my fishing ability and lack of trout!! Feel free to add or subtract ingredients according to your own taste and appetite. Enjoy!

Melt butter in a large skillet over medium heat, add the beaten eggs, salt and pepper and cook until firm. Flip the entire egg mixture and within 5 seconds flip back. Add the cheese, tomatoes, cooked sausage and jalapeno peppers. Flip omelette halfway over, enclosing ingredients in the omelette. Cook until golden brown. Roll the prepared omelette in a large tortilla with the sliced avocado. Serve with salsa and sour cream. Serves 1 to 2.

Dick Anderson

Monday Night Garbanzo Bean Soup

4   slices bacon
1/2   head cabbage, shredded
1   bay leaf,
1   onion, chopped
4   garlic cloves, minced
       Black pepper to taste
2   8 ounce cans tomato sauce
1   cup water,
4   potatoes, cubed
2   15-ounce cans garbanzo beans
1   cup ham, cubed

• •

Fry bacon until crispy, then cut into small pieces. Add cabbage to bacon and fry together about 10 minutes, stirring until cabbage is cooked down and partially translucent. Transfer to a large saucepan. Add bay leaf, onion, garlic and pepper to cabbage mixture. Stir in tomato sauce and water. Cook for 15 to 20 minutes. Add potatoes, beans and ham. Cook until potatoes are done and soup is thick. Serves 6 to 8.

Nick Buoniconti's SPRITE Cake

1-1/2   cups butter or margarine
3   cups granulated sugar
5   eggs, beaten
3   cups all-purpose flour
3/4   cup Sprite beverage
2   teaspoons lemon flavoring
1   teaspoon vanilla extract

Combine butter with sugar. Add eggs. Add one flour one cup at a time. Beat until thick. Then add Sprite, lemon flavoring and vanilla. Pour into a lightly greased and floured bundt cake pan. Bake at 325 degrees F for one hour and 15 minutes. Cool. Turn cake out upside-down to serve.

Nick Buoniconti

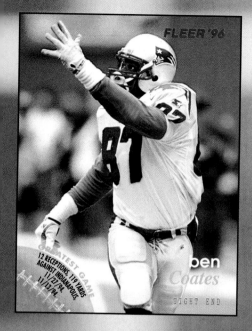

Sure Handed Barbecue Ribs

2	pound rack pork ribs
2	tablespoons brown sugar
1/2	cup ketchup
1	tablespoon lemon juice
1	teaspoon salt
1	teaspoon garlic butter
3	tablespoons dry mustard
1	teaspoon cold water

• •

Preheat oven 400 degrees F. Rub brown sugar into ribs.
Mix remaining ingredients and coat ribs with mixture.
Bake for 1-1/4 hours at 400 degrees F., basting often with
any extra marinade. Serves 3 to 4.

Black, White, Lemon and Strawberry Cookies

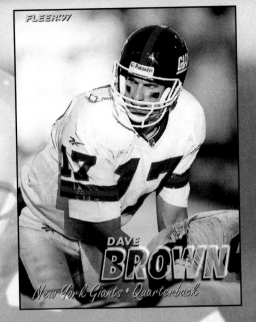

FLEER97

DAVE BROWN

New York Giants • Quarterback

1-3/4 cups of granulated sugar
4   large eggs (at room temperature)
1   cup of milk
2   sticks of unsalted butter (at room temperature)
1   teaspoon of vanilla extract
1/2   teaspoon lemon extract
1   teaspoon baking powder
3/4   teaspoon salt
2-1/2 cups of flour
2-1/2 cups of cake flour

Frosting:
1   box (16 ounces) of confectioners sugar with white, black, lemon and strawberry extract (as desired)
1/2   cup of boiling water

• •

Notes: You can make the dough chocolate by putting 1/3 to cup of cocoa powder into the flour. Almond extract can be added for additional flavor, or can be substituted for vanilla. Confectioners sugars in chocolate, white, strawberry and lemon are made by Domino sugar.

Preheat the oven to 375 degrees F. Butter or bakers spray, 2 or 3 baking sheets and set aside.

Combine sugar and butter in bowl of electric mixer and whip until fluffy. Add eggs, milk, vanilla and lemon extract and mix until smooth.

In a large bowl, combine flours, baking powder and salt. Stir until mixed. Gradually add dry ingredients to butter mixture. Stir well to combine. Drop dough by the tablespoon, approximately two inches apart on the baking sheets. Bake until edges begin to brown. 25 to 30 minutes. Allow to cool completely.

To make frosting, divide sugar into 4 bowls (about 1 1/8 cups each), add about 2 tablespoons boiling water to one bowl. Stir constantly until the mix is thick and spreadable. Then add boiling water to next bowl, etc. Add any color extracts desired to any of the bowls.

With a small brush, frost one side of cookie, then brush the other side with the color you desire.

2	bell peppers, seeded and chopped
2 to 3	stalks celery, chopped
1	large onion, chopped
1	stick margarine
3 to 4	10-ounce cans condensed cream of mushroom soup
2	can Rotel tomatoes, undrained (or Cajun tomatoes if Rotel unavailable
2	1-pound packages crawfish tails (may substitute shrimp

Too Hot Too Handle Crawfish Ettouffe

Saute bell peppers, celery and onion in margarine until soft.

Add the soup and cook for 20 to 30 minutes. Add the crawfish tails and cook 30 to 40 more minutes. Add the tomatoes and cook until heated through. Serve over rice. Serves 6.

Mike Holmgren, my coach and I make a great team. Sometimes after practice or an intense film session, he lets me cook up some of my favorite hometown bayou recipes. It took a while for Mike to get the crawfish, but now he loves the dish. Mike is still a burgerman himself.

Brett Favre

Cris & Melanie Carter Endzone Oxtail Soup

4-6   pound oxtails
2   6-ounce cans tomato sauce
       Salt and pepper to taste
3   cups freshly cut mixed vegetables
3   cups freshly cut carrots
3   16-ounce cans corn

• • • • • • • • • • • • • • • • • • •

Put oxtails in a large pot and cook on medium-low heat until just tender. Add tomato sauce and salt and pepper to taste. Add mixed vegetables, carrots and corn. Let soup simmer for 45 minutes. Serve hot and enjoy. Serves 8 to 10.

A long time ago, slaves were bought by slave owners to work for them. Slaves would collect food and slaughter animals for their masters' feasts. Slave owners were always fed the prime cuts of beef and fresh vegetables. Slaves were given the scraps from slaughtered animals and rotten crops. Naturally, the slave owners did not want to eat the oxtails so they were given to the slaves. Slaves would take the oxtails and make this tasty soup. Our families have been making oxtail soup for years. We are proud to have passed this tradition on to our children and now to you. We wish you a wonderful holiday season.

Cooked with Love,
The Carter Family

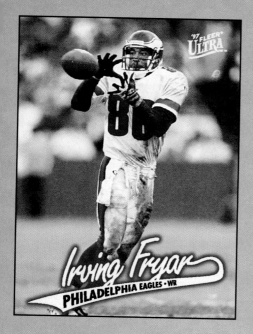

Heavenly Peach Cobbler Delight

2	cups sliced fresh peaches
2	cups sugar
1/2	cup butter
1-1/2	cups flour
2	teaspoons baking powder
1/4	teaspoon salt
3/4	cup milk

Preheat oven to 350 degrees F. Place peaches and 1 cup sugar in a medium-sized bowl. Stir gently until blended, then set aside.

Place butter in a 2-quart casserole and place in oven to melt. Combine remaining sugar, flour, baking powder, salt and milk in mixing bowl. Stir mixture with wooden spoon to blend. Remove casserole from oven. Pour batter over melted butter, but do NOT stir. Spoon peaches over the batter. Bake for 60 minutes or until batter rises and turns golden brown. Serves 6.

Downfield Fettuccine With Three-Cheese Sauce

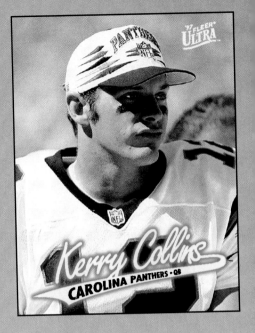

1-1/2 pounds spinach fettuccine
1-1/2 cups milk
1/2   cup heavy cream
1/2   cup grated Parmesan cheese
4   ounces Italian fontina cheese, shredded
1   cup frozen peas, partially thawed
1/4   teaspoon salt
1/8   teaspoon pepper
1/8   teaspoon ground nutmeg
3   ounces blue cheese, crumbled
1/3   cup chopped walnuts, toasted

. . . .

Cook fettuccine in a large saucepot of salted, boiling water for 10 minutes or until al dente. Drain and keep warm.

While pasta is cooking, heat milk and heavy cream in a large skillet over low heat. Gradually add Parmesan and fontina cheeses, stirring with fork or wire whisk about 4 minutes until melted. Stir in peas, salt, pepper and nutmeg. Cook 1 minute or until peas are heated through.

Add blue cheese to sauce, warm for 30 seconds and add pasta to skillet, gently tossing with sauce.

Just before serving, toss walnuts into pasta. (To toast walnuts, place on baking sheet and bake at 350 degrees F 8 minutes or until lightly browned) Serves 6.

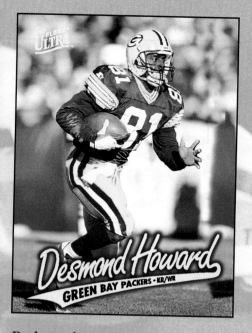

Desmond Howard
GREEN BAY PACKERS · KR/WR

Mom's Breakaway Caramel Cake

2	cups (4 sticks) unsalted butter, at room temperature (plus additional for pans)
3	cups sifted all-purpose flour (plus additional for pans)
1	tablespoon baking powder
1	tablespoon cocoa
2	cups sugar
2	teaspoons vanilla extract
6	large eggs at room temperature
1	cup milk

Preheat the oven to 350 degrees F. Lightly grease and flour three 8-inch round cake pans and set aside. Sift the flour, baking powder and cocoa together and set aside. Cream the butter and the sugar in a bowl with an electric mixer at medium speed until the mixture is light and fluffy. Add the vanilla. Beat in the eggs, one at a time. Change the mixer speed to low and add the dry ingredients alternately with the milk, a little at a time. Mix just until the ingredients are blended. Do Not Over Mix - Cake Will Be Tough.

Divide the batter among the prepared cake pans. Bake until a toothpick inserted into the center of each layer comes out clean, about 20 to 25 minutes. Remove the pans to a wire rack to cool. After about 20 minutes, remove the layers from the pans and let them cool completely on wire racks before frosting. When the layers are completely cool, make the frosting.

Place one layer on a plate and spread it with about one-fourth of the icing. Top with a second layer and spread it with the same amount of icing. Top with the remaining layer. Frost the top and sides of the cake with the remaining icing. Let the cake set at least 30 minutes before serving. Makes 1 8-inch layer cake.

Caramel Icing:

Stir together all ingredients in a medium heavy saucepan over low heat. Cook, stirring constantly, until the sugars are completely dissolved and the icing is thick. To test if the icing is ready, drop 1 teaspoon of icing into a glass of cold water. If icing thickens and forms a soft ball, it is ready.

Note: Do not make icing until the cake is baked and cooled. If icing should get too thick, add a few drops of hot water and mix well.

Caramel Icing:

1	cup (2 sticks) unsalted butter, cut into pieces
1	pound light brown sugar
1	cup granulated sugar
1	12-ounce can evaporated milk

Boomer's BBQ Beef Brisket

4   pounds beef brisket
2   18 ounce bottles Boomer's Heroes
     Original BBQ Sauce*
     Seasoning salt
     Black pepper
     Salt
     Granulated garlic
     Liquid to cover beef while braising

Trim fat from brisket and rub with seasonings. Smoke brisket until beef reaches 110 degrees F. Place brisket in a braising pan and add generous amount of beef stock, slowly braising brisket on low heat until the meat shreds, 1-1 1/2 hours. Add more liquid as needed during cooking. Shred the meat, and add Boomer's BBQ Sauce and serve. Serves 8.

Proceeds from each purchase benefit the Boomer Esiason Heroes Foundation, supporting a cure for Cystic Fibrosis.

17

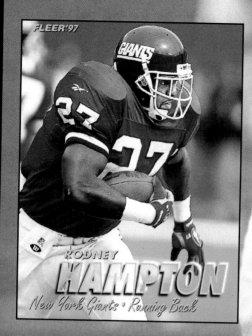

Rodney Hampton's Baked Chicken

1   3 pound chicken, cut into serving-size pieces
2   tablespoons ground black pepper
1   scallion, chopped
1   onion, chopped
2   tablespoons Lawry's seasoning sauce
1   cup (or to taste) bottled barbecue sauce

Place chicken in a baking pan. Add the pepper, scallion, onion and seasoning sauce. Bake at 350 degrees F. for 30 minutes. Add barbecue sauce to taste. Bake, another 20 minutes or until tender. Serves 4.

Brash-talking wide receiver Keyshawn Johnson and hard-nosed fullback Lorenzo Neal are two young, confident players coach Bill Parcells will look to in rebuilding the New York Jets.

Rose Bowl Enchiladas al la Keyshawn

1	pound ground turkey or chicken	1/2	pound mozzarella cheese, grated
1/2	cup chopped onion	1	dozen corn tortillas
1/4	cup chopped green bell pepper		32-ounce can green chili enchilada sauce, warmed
	Lawry's seasoned salt to taste		Sour cream
	Black pepper to taste		Guacamole
1	pound cheddar cheese, grated		

Place the ground turkey, onion, bell pepper, seasoned salt and pepper to taste in a skillet. Sauté until meat is browned, breaking it up into small pieces as you cook. Mix the cheeses and set aside 1/4 cup. Warm tortillas in skillet (using 1 teaspoon vegetable oil if desired). Dip a tortilla in enchilada sauce and place on a plate. Place some ground turkey mixture and cheese in the center of the tortilla. Roll tortilla and place in rectangular pan. Repeat until all 12 enchiladas have been rolled and placed in pan. Pour remaining enchilada sauce over the top. Sprinkle on remaining cheese. Bake in oven at 350 degrees F. 20 to 30 minutes, or until heated through and bubbling. Garnish with sour cream and guacamole. Serve with Spanish rice and green salad. Serves 6.

Keyshawn Joh—

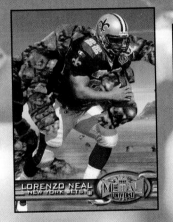

Broiled Fish With Seafood Sauce

Stock:

		Fish:	
	Shrimp heads from 1/2 to 1 pound shrimp	4-6	fish fillets (about 1-1/2 pounds trout, snapper, red fish, or other)
2	small onions, quartered		
4	cups water		Salt and Pepper to taste
2	tablespoons Season-All		Juice of 1 medium lemon
2	teaspoons Cajun Seafood Boil (optional)		

Sauce:

2	tablespoons butter or margarine	2	tablespoons chopped parsley	1	pound crawfish (optional)
1/2	cup onion, finely chopped	2	cloves garlic, minced	1/4	cup white wine
1/3	cup green pepper, finely chopped	1-1/2	cups shrimp stock (above)	1/4	cup milk
1	teaspoon Season-All	1/2	pound small shrimp, peeled and deveined	1	tablespoon flour
		12	ounces lump crabmeat (picked over)		Salt and pepper to taste

To make the stock: place shrimp heads, onions, water, Season-All and Seafood Boil in large pot. Bring to a boil and cook over medium high heat for 15 minutes. Strain and discard solids. Use stock in sauce recipe. Excess stock can be frozen. Makes about 3 cups. For the sauce: heat butter in a large pan over medium heat. Add the onion, green peppers, Season-All and parsley and saute until onions are transparent. Add the garlic and stock, cook 5 minutes. Add the shrimp, crabmeat, crawfish and wine. Cook, stirring occasionally, 5 to 7 minutes, or until shrimp and crawfish are pink. Stir in the milk, flour and salt and pepper to taste. Cook 5 minutes, or until thickened. Pour over broiled fish and serve. To make the fish: place fillets in pan. Season with salt and pepper and pour lemon juice over fish. Marinate in refrigerator for 10 minutes. Broil on bottom rack for 5 to 10 minutes (depending on thickness of fillet) until fish is done and flakes easily with fork. Transfer to platter and top with sauce.

Serves 4 to 6.

Lorenzo Neal

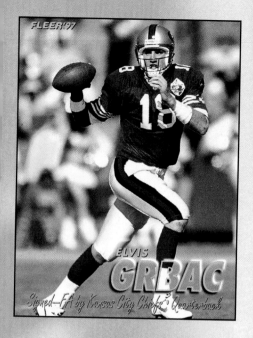

8	ounces sliced mushrooms
1	large red pepper, seeded and coarsely chopped
1	large green pepper, seeded and coarsely chopped
10	scallions, chopped
1	large onion, diced
1	clove garlic, minced
3	large shallots, minced
1/2	cup fresh basil, chopped
2	tablespoons fresh oregano, chopped
	Dash ground red pepper
1/4	cup olive oil
4	cups canned tomatoes, chopped
	Dash salt and pepper
1	pound fusillo, cooked according to package directions and drained
2	tablespoons chopped parsley

Sauté first 10 ingredients in olive oil until lightly browned. Add tomatoes and bring to a boil. Simmer for 20 minutes, stirring occasionally. Season with salt and pepper. Serve over cooked pasta. Garnish with parsley. Serves 4.

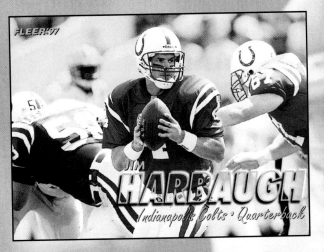

2   1-pound trout or sea bass
       Salt and freshly ground
       pepper to taste
1   lemon, sliced thin
       Fresh thyme leaves

Captain Comeback's Grilled Fish

Clean fish well. Make a slit in center of fish but do not cut all the way through. Sprinkle cavity with salt and pepper. Place half the lemon slices and half the thyme in each fish. Wrap well in aluminum foil and grill over charcoal until, tender about 10 to 12 minutes. Turn once during cooking time. Serves 2 to 4.

Jim Harbaugh

Super Bowl Spinach Ricotta Ravioli With Oven-Dried Tomatoes and Balsamic Reduction

Cooking is my way of relaxing, and a chance f
Jen and me to talk about what happened
throughout the day. I try a few different things
here and there, but I'm a pretty basic cook—I g
for the old standards. Probably my all-time
favorite would be my mother's ravioli. Jen mak
such unbelievable pizzas and pastas and fresh
sauces that I've been trying to talk her into ope
ing a small restaurant. We both enjoy eating an
we both enjoy cooking. I have made these
raviolis ever since I remember being in th
kitchen with my mom. I grew up eating th
best italian food. Through the years, I
developed many favorite sauces, such as
this one. This is healthy and a great mea

Stuffing:
2   pounds cleaned spinach
1/4   cup minced shallot
2   cups ricotta cheese
2   egg yolks
       Salt and pepper to taste

Saute spinach and shallot to wilt spinach.
Put mixture on a towel to drain completely
and let cool. Place in a bowl, chop, and
add ricotta and egg yolks. Season with salt
and pepper.

Balsamic reduction:
12   ounces balsamic vinegar
1   teaspoon sugar

Place in medium saucepan. Reduce over
medium heat to exactly half.

Oven-dried tomatoes:
8   Roma tomatoes, halved and seeded
6   ounces extra virgin olive oil
       Salt and freshly ground pepper
       to taste

Drizzle half the oil over a baking sheet.
Place tomatoes on sheet, cut side down.
Drizzle each tomato with remaining oil,
salt and fresh cracked pepper. Bake at
275 degrees F. for 1 hour. Set aside
when done, and reserve any oil.

Pasta:
4   sheets fresh pasta, approximately
       5 x 12 inches
1   egg yolk beaten with a few drops
       of water

Cut pasta into 36 2-inch circles. Keep
pasta covered with damp cloth while
working so it doesn't dry out. If preferred
buy 18 ready-made unfilled raviolis.

To build raviolis, lay out 1 pasta circle.
Rub edges with egg yolk mixture with tip
of finger just to barely coat. Place 1 tablespoon spinach stuffing in center of pasta.
Then place a second piece on top.

Seal carefully with fingertips, being carefu
to keep stuffing in center of ravioli. Do no
trap air inside. Place on dry plate dusted
with flour. When finished, freeze raviolis
for at least 1 hour.

Cook in salted water at medium boil for 3
to 4 minutes. Place 4 ravioli on each of 4
plates (there are 2 extra ravioli for bigger
appetites) and surround with 4 tomato
halves. Top with oil reserved from tomatoes, about 1 tablespoon per plate, and 1
tablespoon balsamic reduction. Top with
chopped chives or parsley. Makes 18
ravioli; serves 4.

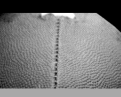

Dan's Shotgun Ribs

1/4 cup Hungarian paprika
1/8 cup kosher salt
1/4 cup granulated sugar
1/2 cup light brown sugar
1/8 cup ground cumin
1/4 cup chili powder
1/8 cup coarsely ground black pepper
3-5 pounds ribs

• • • • • • • • • • • • • • • • • •

Mix all the rub ingredients together well, rub on both sides of beef or pork ribs. Marinate at least 2 hours and grill as desired. Makes 2 cups rub.

I may have bad knees, but my Ribs are great!

BBQ Sauce

2 tablespoons soybean oil
1 large Spanish onion, chopped
1 tablespoon chopped garlic
1 cup plus 2 tablespoons cider vinegar
1 cup plus 2 tablespoons cooking sherry
  cup plus 1 tablespoon light brown sugar
1 pound jar honey
1 tablespoon fresh oregano leaves
6 tablespoons lemon juice
7 tablespoons molasses
1 tablespoon plus 1 teaspoon Rib Rub (see Shotgun Ribs)
6 tablespoons Worcestershire sauce
1/2 cup tomato sauce
2 cups ketchup
3/4 cup chicken stock
3 tablespoons tomato paste
1/3 cup chipotle
3 tablespoons liquid smoke

Heat oil in heavy kettle or Dutch oven. Add onion and garlic and saute until caramelized. Add vinegar, sherry and brown sugar. Cook uncovered, stirring, until reduced by half. Add remaining ingredients and cook for 50 minutes over low heat, stirring occasionally. Puree and use as desired. Makes about 4 quarts.

13

Fresh From The Fridge Red Velvet Cake

with Pecans and Cream Cheese Icing

Cake:
1-1/2 cups sugar
2-1/2 cups cake flour
1   teaspoon baking soda
1   teaspoon cocoa
1-1/2 tablespoons vegetable oil
2   eggs
1   cup buttermilk
1   teaspoon vinegar
1   teaspoon vanilla
1   bottle red food coloring

Frosting:
1-1/2 boxes confectioner's sugar
     (24 ounces)
8   ounces cream cheese
1   stick (1/4 pound) margarine
1-1/2 teaspoons vanilla
1-1/2 cups chopped pecans

Preheat oven to 350 degrees F. Grease and flour 2 8- or 9-inch cake pans and set aside. Sift all dry ingredients 4 times. Beat oil, eggs, buttermilk, vinegar, vanilla and food coloring together well. Beat the dry ingredients into the liquids, one cup at a time. Bake at 350 degrees F. until a toothpick inserted in center of cake comes out clean, about 30 minutes.

Let cool, then remove from pans.

For the frosting, beat the sugar, cream cheese, margarine and vanilla together until fluffy and well mixed. Blend in the chopped pecans. Makes enough to fill and frost 1 8- or 9-inch 2-layer cake.

Perfect Spiral Penne Pasta with Tomatoes, Leeks and Grilled Portobello Mushrooms

My wife, actress Holly Robinson-Peete, and I love this pasta. It was given to us by one of our favorite chefs, John Gray at the Grand Havana Room.

10	ounces olive oil
1	cup balsamic vinegar
8	ounces portobello mushrooms, stems removed
6	ounces leek, halved lengthwise, cut in twin half circles, cleaned in cold water and drained
1	pound tomatoes, cut in 1-inch pieces
	Salt and freshly ground pepper to taste
1	pound cooked penne pasta, drained
4	ounces unsalted butter
4	ounces grated Parmesan cheese

• •

Mix 1 cup of the olive oil and the balsamic vinegar. Add the mushrooms and marinate for 30 minutes. Grill until soft, approximately 3 minutes per side. Let cool, then cut into 1-inch pieces.

Saute the mushrooms, leek and tomatoes on high heat in remaining 2 tablespoons olive oil. Season with salt and pepper. Allow liquid in pan to reduce by half. Add cooked pasta. Reduce heat. Add butter and half the grated Parmesan. Stir constantly, until butter and cheese have melted and become creamy. Remove from heat add salt to taste. Serve topped with remaining Parmesan and ground pepper. Serves 4.

Rodney Peete

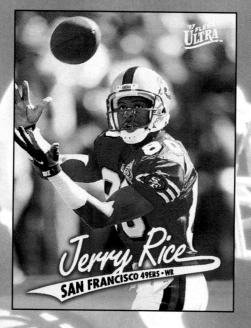

Record Breaking Risotto With Broccoli Rabe and Garlic

4	cloves garlic
2	sprigs fresh rosemary
1/4	teaspoon crushed red pepper
5-1/2	cups chicken broth, defatted
2	teaspoons olive oil
1	red bell pepper, seeded and diced
1	onion, finely chopped
1	cup Arborio rice
1	bunch broccoli rabe (rapini), stemmed and coarsely chopped (if desired, substitute Swiss chard)
2/3	cup freshly grated Parmesan cheese Salt and freshly ground black pepper to taste

My teammates are always looking for a free meal and this is one I don't mind serving up to a group of hungry critics. It's healthy and delicious and works for me.

• •

Wrap garlic, rosemary and crushed pepper in cheesecloth. Put in a 3-quart saucepan, add broth and bring to a boil over medium heat. Reduce heat to low and simmer for 10 minutes.

In a large skillet, heat oil over medium heat, add bell pepper and onion and cook, until softened, 4 to 6 minutes. Stir in rice and cook, stirring, for 1 minute.

Ladle in 1/2 cup of simmering broth and cook, stirring frequently, until most of the liquid has been absorbed, about 1 minute. Continue stirring and adding broth as it is absorbed, 1/2 cup at a time, until only 1 cup broth remains, about 15 minutes total.

Stir in broccoli rabe and remaining broth. Cook, stirring, until the rice is just tender and the mixture is creamy, 5 to 7 minutes. Remove from heat and stir in Parmesan. Season with salt and pepper. Serve hot.

Jerry Rice

Third & Long Tenderloin Kabob

2	pounds your favorite boneless meat (lamb, beef or veal)
1	large onion, peeled and sliced
4	cloves garlic, peeled and crushed
1/2	teaspoon freshly ground black pepper
3/4	cup fresh lime juice
2	teaspoons salt
1/4	teaspoon ground saffron, dissolved in 1 tablespoon hot water
1	cup low-fat unflavored yogurt
8	cherry tomatoes or 2 large tomatoes, quartered
8	mushrooms
1	green or red pepper, seeded and cut into 8 squares
2	tablespoons olive oil
	Juice of 2 limes (additional)
1	teaspoon salt

Trim all fat and gristle from meat and cut into large cubes. Place meat in a large non-reactive container. Add onion, garlic, pepper, lime juice, salt, saffron and yogurt to the container. Mix well. Cover the meat and marinate for at least 24 hours in refrigerator, turning occasionally.

Start charcoal on a grill and while it is heating, thread each piece of meat onto skewers, leaving a few inches free on both ends. Thread tomatoes mushrooms and peppers together on separate skewers.

Combine oil, the juice of 2 limes, and 1 teaspoon salt in a small saucepan. Keep warm. When coals are ready, brush the vegetables and meat lightly with the oil-lime mixture. Place skewers on grill and cook 3 to 4 minutes on each side, turning the skewers often. The meat should be seared on the outside, pink and juicy in the inside. Serve with rice and, if desired, Persian flatbread. Serves 4.

Move the Chains Cornbread

1-3/4 cups white corn meal
1/2   cup flour
3   tablespoons sugar
1   teaspoon salt
1   egg
2   tablespoons baking powder
1-1/2 cups buttermilk
1/3   cup Crisco oil

• •

Preheat 400 Degrees F. Heat oil in 8 1/8 x 2 frying pan, mix all ingredients except the oil, pour hot oil on top of mixture, stir all ingredients, pour into Pyrex pan and bake for 20 minutes.

These recipes are very dear to me because they represent family tradition. This recipe was first created by my grandmother then passed on to my mom. My shrimp is a personal favorite that I renamed after one of Pittsburgh's three rivers.

Catch-Of-The-Day Monongahela Shrimp

3   tablespoons olive oil
3   red onions, quartered
8   new potatoes, quartered
6   cloves garlic, chopped
1   teaspoon crushed red pepper

3   dashes Tabasco sauce
2   pounds shrimp, peeled and deveined
1   pound pasta (your choice), cooked according to package directions and drained

Heat olive oil in a large skillet. Add the onions, potatoes and garlic and saute until all is tender. Add the red pepper, Tabasco sauce and shrimp and cook until shrimp is done. Serve over pasta and enjoy! Serves 4.

Franco's Immaculate Baked Lasagna

3   large cloves garlic
1   pound ground round steak
1   28-ounce can tomato puree
1   large onion
1   6-ounce can tomato paste,
     plus 1 can water
1/2   teaspoon oregano
1/4   teaspoon basil
1/4   cup red wine
     Salt to taste
1/2   cup fresh Romano cheese,
     grated
1   pound lasagna noodles,
     cooked according to package
     directions and drained
1   pound ricotta cheese
8   ounces mozzarella

Preheat oven to 350 degrees F. Lightly grease a 9 x 13-inch baking pan. Chop garlic very fine and brown in a large skillet, along with the meat (which you should crumble into tiny pieces). Drain off excess grease.

Combine tomato puree and onion in a food processor or blender until smooth. Add this to the meat, along with the tomato paste, water, oregano, basil, red wine and salt. Cover and simmer for 10 minutes.

Cover bottom of pan with one-third of the meat mixture. Grate one-third of the Romano over this. Lay 5 lasagna noodles lengthwise and 1 crosswise at top to fill pan. Top with one-third each of the ricotta and mozzarella. Repeat layers twice more, using only 5 noodles in each of the remaining layers. Bake at 350 degrees F. for 30 minutes. Serves 6 to 8.

Franco Harris

Junior Seau

A monster at middle linebacker, Junior Seau has been named to the Pro Bowl after every season since 1991. He also led the San Diego Chargers to Super Bowl XXIX following the 1994 season.

Goal Line Stand Cheese Filled Tortellini with Blackened Chicken and Chipotle Cream Sauce

1	whole boneless chicken breas[t]
4	tablespoons Cajun blackened spice
2	tablespoons olive oil
1/2	teaspoon garlic, chopped fine
1	teaspoon cilantro, chopped fin[e]
1	tomato, diced
1	roasted pasilla chili, diced
1/4	cup white wine
1/2	cup heavy cream
3	tablespoons Chipotle Mayonnaise (below)
6	ounces cheese-filled cooked, drained tortellini
1/2	teaspoon unsalted butter
	Salt and pepper to taste

Chipotle Mayonnaise

2	tablespoons mayonnaise
1-1/2	teaspoons BBQ sauce
1/2	teaspoon black pepper
1/2	teaspoon salt
1	teaspoon minced garlic
1-1/2	teaspoons canned chipotle chilies, pureed into a smooth paste
2	tablespoons Worcestershire sauce

Combine all ingredients and blend i[n] a food processor. Makes about 3 tablespoons.

Spread blackened spice on a plate and dredge chicken, coating both sides. Saute in a hot pan, leaving chicken in the pan long enough to "blacken" the spices and to cook the chicken through. Cool the chicken and cut into 1/2-inch dice.

In a saute pan, heat olive oil. Add garlic and saute briefly. Add the cilantro, tomato, diced chili, and chicken. Saute for 2 minutes, then add white wine and cook over high heat, scraping down sides and reducing mixture until wine is almost gone. Lower heat and add cream and chipotle mayonnaise, season with salt and pepper to taste. Reduce until your sauce is desired consistency, and stir in butter. Serve with tortellini. Serves 2.

Lone Star Chicken Lasagna

Hey, if all I ate were milkshakes every day, I'd look like Nate Newton. I really love my original Chicken Lasagna, it's tasty and gives me the energy to run around on Sunday afternoons.

2	cups shredded mozzarella cheese
1	16-ounce box lasagna noodles, cooked according to package directions and drained

Chicken Sauce:

6-8	skinless, boneless chicken breast halves
1	medium onion, chopped
1	tablespoon vegetable oil
	Salt and pepper to taste
2	tablespoons oregano
1	tablespoon garlic powder
2	6-ounce cans tomato paste
1	cup hot water
1	4-ounce can chopped mushrooms

Cheese Mixture:

2	cups small curd cottage cheese
1/2	cup grated Parmesan cheese
1	tablespoon parsley flakes
1	egg, beaten

Combine all ingredients and mix well.

• •

Cut-up chicken breast into bite-sized pieces. Saute chicken and onion in the oil. Add remaining ingredients and simmer for 30 minutes.

• •

Pour 1/2 cup sauce on bottom of 13 x 9 x 2-inch baking dish. Arrange one-third of the noodles over the sauce. Top with one-third remaining chicken sauce, one-third the cottage cheese mixture and two-thirds cup mozzarella. Repeat twice more, ending with the remaining mozzarella on top. Preheat oven to 375 Degrees F. Cover pan with foil. Bake 35 to 40 minutes. Let stand 10 minutes before cutting. Serves 10.

Bulldog Chicken Casserole

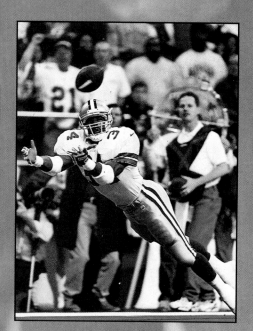

4	cups diced cooked chicken
2	cups corn bread stuffing mix
2	cups herb stuffing mix
1	can cream of mushroom soup
1	can cream of chicken soup
4	cups chicken broth
1	small onion
1	stick butter

• •

Melt butter, mix with 2 cups of broth, and toss with stuffing mixes; set aside. In blender, combine soups, remaining broth and onion. Blend until onion is chopped and mixture is well combined.

Grease 9 x 13-inch baking dish. Place a layer of stuffing, layer of chicken and pour 1/2 of soup mix over. Repeat. Be sure to save 1 cup of stuffing mix to sprinkle over top. Bake in 350 degrees F. oven 30 to 45 minutes. Serves 6 to 8.

Quarterback Jeff Blake and tight end Tony McGee, both 26, are key members of the Cincinnati Bengals youth movement. Blake has already played in the Pro Bowl, and McGee has averaged 44 catches per season.

Goin' Deep Baked Stuffed Mushrooms

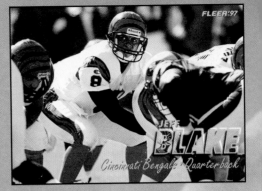

1   8 ounce package cream cheese
3/4 cup freshly grated Parmesan cheese
1/4 cup bacon bits
2   cloves garlic, minced
2   cups medium size mushroom caps
1   cup shredded mild cheddar cheese

Preheat oven to 375 degrees F. Blend cream cheese, Parmesan, bacon bits and garlic. Spoon a tablespoon of mixture into each mushroom cap. Arrange in baking pan and bake 20 minutes at 375 degrees F. Sprinkle with cheddar cheese and bake until melted.

Serve hot. Serves 4 to 6 as an appetizer.

Button-Hook Garlic Mashed Potatoes

2   pounds red potatoes, quartered
1   teaspoon fresh thyme leaves, minced
1/2 cup (approximately) milk
2   tablespoons butter or margarine
1/2 teaspoon garlic powder
    Salt, pepper and seasoned salt to taste

Put the potatoes and fresh thyme in a heavy saucepan. Add water to cover and boil together until soft. Drain the potatoes and add milk (enough to cover the bottom of the pot).

Let simmer 5 to 10 minutes on low heat. Add butter or margarine, garlic powder, salt, pepper, and seasoned salt. Mash well and serve. Serves 4.

Time-Out for Mom's Chocolate Chip Cookies

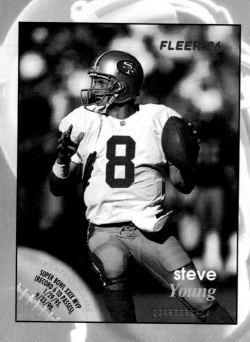

4	cups all-purpose flour
3/4	cups quick oatmeal
2	teaspoons baking soda
2	teaspoons salt
2	cups Crisco Shortening
1-1/2	cups granulated sugar
1-1/2	cups packed brown sugar
2	teaspoons vanilla extract
4	large eggs
4	cups Nestle Toll House chocolate morsels

Nuts are optional

For the really brave, my favorite Cookie Sandwich (not mother approved!) is to take two cookies, warm from the oven, and place a tablespoon of raw cookie dough in between, they are delicious!

Combine flour, oatmeal, baking soda and salt in small bowl. Beat shortening granulated sugar, brown sugar and vanilla in a large mixing bowl. Add eggs one at a time to sugar mixture, beating well after each addition. Gradually beat in flour mixture. Stir in morsels and nuts. Drop by tablespoon onto ungreased baking sheets. Bake in preheated 375 degree F. oven for 9 to 11 minutes or until golden brown. Let stand for 2 minutes, then remove to wire racks to cool completely. Makes about 10 dozen cookies.

Steve Young
49ers

Some call our Super Bowl win destiny. I call it 29 years overdue. But building a great team takes time. So does building a strong body. With 9 essential nutrients, milk can help. Just stay with it. Every day. Because as my teammates will tell you, being the best doesn't happen overnight.

MILK

Where's *your* mustache?℠

Stop and Pop Fettucine

1	pound noodles
3/4	cup butter, melted
1-1/2	cups heavy cream
1/2	cup grated Romano cheese
1/2	cup grated Parmesan
	Ground pepper to taste

Begin cooking pasta in salted, boiling water. Bring mixture of butter and heavy cream to a boil, stirring constantly.

Add the cheese by sprinkling into mixture while stirring constantly until the cheeses have melted and the mixture appears glossy. Add pepper.

Add sauce to the hot noodles that have been cooked to your preferred texture. Serve immediately. This dish cannot be held because it begins to separate. Serves 4.

John Havlicek

"Hondo" won eight championships with the Boston Celtics, popularizing the role of the sixth-man. He scored at least 1,000 points in each of his 16 seasons and averaged 20.8 points per game for his career.

Bounce Pass Lamb Chops A La Cousy

My wife, Marie, developed this recipe which tends to provide more juice to make gravy. Our family has always liked a gravy for meat, potatoes and even sometimes the vegetables! Lamb, when cooked the traditional way, can be very dry. It's one of our favorite meals.

8	thick lean lamb chops	1/8	teaspoon pepper
1	teaspoon garlic oil (homemade if possible)	1/4	teaspoon oregano
1	tablespoon mint jelly	1	onion, sliced thinly
1/4	teaspoon salt	1/4	teaspoon Gravy Master

The preparation to marinate these chops begins as soon as you get them home from the grocer. My wife, Marie, makes her own garlic oil by simply peeling several garlic cloves and putting them into a small jar of fresh olive oil. She leaves this in the refrigerator and just continues to add oil as needed.

Rub the chops with the garlic oil and then add a little mint jelly over the top of the chops. Use about 1/8 teaspoon per chop or to taste.

Marinate in refrigerator for two to three hours. Let the meat come to room temperature before baking. If the chops are not going to be used for that day's meal, freeze each chop individually by wrapping in plastic wrap. As the meat defrosts it will be marinating.

In a shallow casserole dish, add enough water to cover the bottom and season lightly with Gravy Master, to add color. Place the chops into the casserole dish, sprinkled with salt, pepper and oregano and then place an onion slice on top of each lamb chop. Cover the dish and place into a preheated 350 degree oven. Immediately turn the oven down to 300 degrees and bake for about an hour. Check to see that chops are tender.

When chops are tender remove from the casserole and put into a broiling pan. Broil the chops just long enough to brown slightly. Save the juices from the casserole to prepare your gravy. Serves 8.

The orchestrator of six Boston Celtics titles, Cousy totaled 6,955 assists and averaged more than 18 points per game during a Hall-of-Fame career that spanned from 1950-1969.

Showtime Chicken Cordon Bleu

Bryant

2   whole chicken breasts, boned and skinned
1/2   cup cooked ham, minced
1/2   cup cheddar cheese, grated
1/2   cup all-purpose flour
     Salt and black pepper to taste
1   egg
3   tablespoons flour
1   cup bread crumbs
6   cups peanut oil

• •

Cut each chicken breast in half and remove tendons. One at a time, place breast halves between two sheets of waxed paper and pound flat.

Combine minced ham and grated cheese with hands. Form into four rolls to fit in middle of a flattened breast half (about 3 inches long). Place a roll on each breast half and fold breast half around it, beginning with one long side, then short sides, finishing with a long side - like an envelope. Press edges together and roll each piece as it is finished in a sheet of waxed paper.

Season flour with salt and pepper. Beat egg lightly with 1 teaspoon water. Line up a plate with flour, a shallow dish with beaten egg, and a plate with bread crumbs. One by one, roll each piece in flour to coat, then dip in egg, coating completely, and roll in bread crumbs, pressing crumbs into egg coating. Place chicken pieces on a tray and refrigerate for one hour. Heat peanut oil in a fryer or wok to 350 degrees. Fry chicken pieces, two at a time, in hot oil, until browned evenly and firm to the touch. Serves 4.

Just 18 years old and fresh out of high school, Bryant provided spark off the bench by averaging 8.7 points per game for the Los Angeles Lakers in 1996-97. He also won the 1997 Slam Dunk Contest during the NBA All-Star Weekend.

Allan
Houston

One of the premier outside shooters in the NBA, Houston has made good on 40.3% of his three-point attempts and averaged 14.4 points per game over four seasons with the Detroit Pistons and New York Knicks.

Buzzer Beater Baked Fish Fillets

1	pound fish fillets
1	teaspoon lemon juice
1/8	teaspoon paprika
	Salt and pepper to taste
1	tablespoon butter
1	tablespoon all-purpose flour
1/2	cup milk
1/4	cup buttered bread crumbs
1	tablespoon snipped parsley

Preheat oven to 350 degrees F. Cut fillets into serving pieces and place in greased shallow baking pan. Sprinkle with lemon juice, paprika, salt and pepper. In saucepan, melt butter. Blend in flour and dash of salt and pepper. Add milk and stir constantly until thickened and bubbly, about 1 minute. Pour sauce over fillets and sprinkle with bread crumbs. Bake at 350 degrees F. for 35 minutes or until golden brown. Serve sprinkled with parsley. Serves 4.

Charlie
Ward

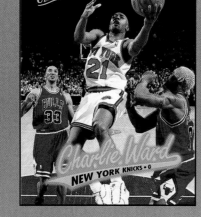

The 1993 Heisman Trophy winner as a quarterback at Florida State, Ward now passes for the New York Knicks as a point guard.

Heisman Low Fat Winter Soup

1-1/2	pounds boneless, skinless chicken breast, cut into strips
1	teaspoon garlic powder
1	teaspoon pepper
1	tablespoon light soy sauce
2	tablespoons olive oil
1	16-ounce package frozen mixed vegetables
1	16-ounce can diced stewed tomatoes, undrained
2	cans water (use tomato can)
1	envelope Lipton Savory Herb with Garlic Soup Mix
2	tablespoons sugar
1	reduced sodium chicken bouillon cube
	Dash lite salt
6	ounces yolk-free noodles

Season chicken with garlic powder, pepper, and soy sauce. Heat oil in skillet and lightly brown chicken. Combine remaining ingredients except noodles in a large pot. Bring to a boil, then simmer on low for about 10 minutes. Add chicken and noodles and simmer until noodles are soft. Serves 5 to 6. Good served with cornbread.

1	4-1/2 pound roasting chicken
3	pounds small red bliss potatoes
2	sprigs fresh rosemary
1	large clove garlic
1/4	teaspoon salt
	Freshly ground pepper to taste
2	tablespoons extra virgin olive oil
3-1/2	tablespoons balsamic vinegar
1/2	teaspoon brown sugar

Balsamic Chicken and "Mash" Potatoes

Rinse chicken and potatoes with cold water. Dry thoroughly inside and out. Mince together rosemary leaves and garlic in salt. Add in the pepper. Rub the olive oil over chicken and potatoes. Rub herb mixture over chicken and potatoes. Refrigerate for several hours, lightly covered with plastic wrap.

When ready to cook, preheat oven to 350 degrees F. Rub any seasoning that may have fallen into the chicken and potatoes. Place chicken breast down in heavy roasting pan and cook 20 to 25 minutes per pound (about 1-3/4 hours). Baste continuously with pan juices. During the last 30 to 45 minutes of cooking turn chicken over to brown the breast. Stir potatoes often during cooking so they don't stick to pan. If necessary, turn heat up for last 10 minutes to brown chicken and potatoes. When chicken is done, blend the balsamic vinegar and brown sugar together and drizzle evenly over chicken and potatoes. Garnish with rosemary sprigs. Serves 6.

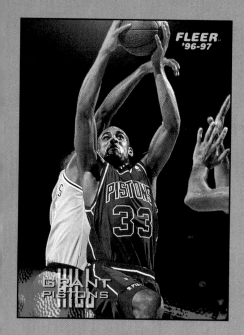

Triple Double New Orleans Gumbo

1-1/2	pounds fresh okra, cut in small pieces or frozen, cut okra
1/2	cup (or more) vegetable oil
1-1/2	pounds fresh shrimp, peeled, deveined and washed
3	boiled crabs (if available)
1	pound crabmeat (claw or white meat)
1/2	pound diced ham (seasoning ham) bite size
1/2	pound Hillshire Beef smoked sausage, cut in bite-size pieces
1-1/2	tablespoons flour
1-1/2	pounds chicken thighs or breast parts, skinned
1	large onion chopped
2	cloves garlic, finely minced
1	green pepper, chopped
2	ribs celery chopped
1/4	cup chopped parsley
2	teaspoons dried thyme
1	large bay leaf
5	cans (14 1/2 oz.) clear chicken broth
2	tablespoons gumbo file, optional

I have been eating Gumbo for the past 24 years. This gumbo recipe is my grandmother's who lives in New Orleans. She always prepares this meal for me. My great grandmother prepared this recipe for the past 55 years. The Cajun gumbo recipe is not a Creole recipe because there are no tomatoes in the soup. It tastes best when using the seafood from the Gulf of Mexico. Some kids might find it too exotic but I love it—especially my grandmothers.

Place cut okra in pot with 1/4 cup oil and saute on medium fire until it is hot, stirring constantly. Reduce heat to low and continue cooking for 45 minutes stirring frequently, as okra tends to stick to bottom of the pot. Stir in flour.

Place chicken in a large pot with enough water to cover. Boil covered for 1 hour.

In separate skillet saute the onion, garlic, and celery in 3 tablespoons of oil, until soft, about 5 minutes. Add chopped green pepper and saute another 2 or 3 minutes.

After the chicken is cooked, remove from pot, reserving cooking liquid, and cut with scissors in bite size pieces. Add canned chicken broth and cooked okra to the pot of cooking liquid. (The okra should be dry at this point.) Bring to a boil and stir to mix the okra with the chicken broth.

Add vegetable mixture, bay leaf and thyme. Cook on low heat about 15 minutes. Add diced ham and boiled crabs, if available. Cook another 15 minutes. Add smoked sausage and boil gently another 15 minutes. Add shrimp and boil another 4 to 5 minutes, depending on size of shrimp. Don't overcook. Add chicken, and crab meat and parsley. Cook 3 minutes. Turn off heat. Add or sprinkle file over gumbo and stir to dissolve. Season with salt, if necessary, to taste. Stir gumbo while cooking. If gumbo is too thick, add additional chicken broth for the desired consistency. Serve over hot cooked rice in a soup bowl. Serves 10 to 12.

Double Dunkin' No-Bake Oatmeal Chocolate Cookies

1   cup sugar
1/2   cup margarine
1/3   cup skim milk
1/2   cup chopped pecans
1/2   cup shredded dried coconut
2   cups quick oats
2   tablespoons candied lemon or
      orange peel
1   cup semi-sweet chocolate morsels
2   tablespoons orange juice

Place the sugar, margarine and milk in a food processor and process until mixture is smooth. Add pecans, coconut, fruit peel, oatmeal, chocolate morsels and orange juice. Process until just mixed, about 5 or 6 seconds. Line 2 cookie sheets with waxed paper. Drop mixture by teaspoon onto waxed paper. Refrigerate at least 1 hour before serving. To store, put into an airtight container and refrigerate. Makes about 3 dozen cookies.

Juwan Howard

Howard had a banner season in 1996-97: he made his first All-Star Game appearance, led the the Washington Bullets with 19.5 points per game and helped his club to their first post-season bid in ten years.

Michael

Jordan

Air Jordan's Carolina Chicken Served Over Fresh Cheddar Biscuits

*This is my family's favorite meal!
I have loved this dish ever since I
played in North Carolina.*

2	tablespoons olive oil
2	cups cubed roast chicken
1	cup diced carrots, blanched
1	cup sliced mushrooms
3/4	cup fresh corn kernels
1/4	cup sautéd diced bacon
1/2	cup chicken stock
2	cups heavy cream
1	tablespoon grain mustard
4	teaspoons fresh chopped parsley
2	teaspoons fresh chopped basil
	Salt and white pepper to taste

Saute vegetables in olive oil until tender. Add chicken, chicken stock, mustard and heavy cream and simmer until thick. Stir in bacon, parsley and basil. Add salt and pepper to taste.

To Serve: Split 4 biscuits in half and place each one on a plate. Ladle the Creamed Chicken over the biscuit and garnish with fresh parsley sprig.

Serves 4.

CHEDDAR BISCUITS

1-1/4	cups flour
1	tablespoon baking powder
1/2	tablespoons salt
1	ounce sugar
3-1/2	ounces butter
1/4	cup whole eggs
1	cup buttermilk
1	cup grated cheddar cheese

Mix dry ingredients together in mixing bowl. Cut butter into small pieces and mix with the dry ingredients. Mix until the butter is the size of small peas. Add eggs, buttermilk and cheese, mix until the dough comes together. Roll out on a floured counter to a 1 inch thickness. Cut into 3-inch round biscuits and bake on a lightly greased baking sheet at 375° for 20 minutes.

Makes 16 biscuits.

In The Paint
Sweet Potato Pie

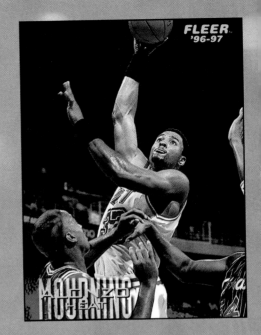

2	9" pie crusts
3	sweet potatoes, boiled until soft, peeled
1/2	cup butter or margarine
2	cups sugar
	Dash salt
6	eggs
2	tablespoons vanilla extract
3/4	tablespoon cinnamon
1/4	teaspoon nutmeg
1	large can evaporated milk

Place potatoes and butter into a mixing bowl and mix on medium speed until combined. Mix in remaining ingredients on medium speed until smooth. Divide mixture into two nine inch pie crusts. Bake at 350° for approximately one hour, or until hot throughout and golden brown on top. Makes 2 pies.

The New York Liberty's Lobo and the Phoenix Mercury's Lieberman Cline bridge two ages of basketball in the WNBA. Lobo was the college player of the year in 1995, and Lieberman Cline won the award in '79 and '80.

Nana Lobo's Chicken

2	teaspoons paprika
2	teaspoons oregano
2	teaspoons garlic powder
2	teaspoons celery salt
3	pound chicken, cut up
2/3 to 1	bottle Catalina salad dressing
1	cup ketchup
3	drops Gravy Master
1/2	cup chopped onion

Mix the paprika, oregano, garlic powder and celery salt and rub on chicken in the same bowl. Mix remaining ingredients. Add chicken, mix, cover with tin foil and marinate in refrigerator until ready to cook.

When ready to cook, place chicken in marinade in shallow baking pan. Cover with foil. Bake 2 hours at 350 degrees F. Remove foil and turn chicken during last hour of baking. Serves 4.

Hoop-It-Up Eggplant Parmigiana

2	eggplants, about 1-1/4 pounds each
2	eggs, lightly beaten
1	cup bread crumbs
3	tablespoons olive oil
1	15-ounce can tomato sauce
1	16-ounce can stewed tomatoes
1	tablespoon basil
1	tablespoon oregano
1	teaspoon garlic powder
	Salt and pepper to taste
1	pound mozzarella cheese, sliced
2	tablespoons minced Italian parsley

Wash and stem eggplants and slice 1/4 inch thick. Dip eggplant slices in eggs and then bread crumbs. Heat oil in skillet and sauté eggplant slices, one layer at a time, until golden brown on both sides. Mix tomato sauce, stewed tomatoes, basil, oregano, garlic powder, and salt and pepper in a medium saucepan and heat. Line a 9-inch x 12-inch baking dish lightly with bread crumbs. Alternate layers of eggplant, cheese and sauce. Top with cheese and sprinkle with parsley.
Bake at 350 degrees F. for 45 minutes or until sauce is bubbly and cheese is melted. Serves 4 to 6.

3	tablespoons oil
2	cups chopped onion
1	15-ounce can tomato sauce
2	16-ounce cans tomatoes, drained and chopped
2	cloves garlic, crushed
1	teaspoon black pepper
1	teaspoon cayenne pepper
2	teaspoons cumin
	Shortening or oil for heating tortillas (about 1/2 cup)
12	flour tortillas
2-1/2	cups grated Monterey jack or cheddar cheese
1/4	cup chopped onion (additional)
1/2	cup chopped green pepper
1	16-ounce can black beans, drained
1/4	cup sliced black olives (optional)
1	cup lowfat sour cream
	paper towels

Sheryl Swoopes' Enchiladas

My favorite food is Mexican. This is an old recipe I have been eating for years. It's great energy food before a game!

• •

Heat 3 tablespoons oil in a large skillet. Add the 2 cups chopped onion and saute until golden. Stir in tomato sauce, tomatoes, garlic, cayenne, black pepper and cumin. Simmer for approximately 20 minutes.

The next steps are easy. Heat the oil or shortening and with tongs dip one tortilla at a time in the hot oil for a few seconds only (do not let them get crispy)! Place the tortilla on the plate with one paper towel underneath and with the other one blot dry. As soon as possible, place 1/4 cup of the sauce down the center of the tortilla in a line. Spoon in 2 tablespoons of black beans. Top with cheese and onion. Now with the edge of the tortillas fold over the sauce and roll the tortilla tightly. Place in a casserole dish that holds at least 12 enchiladas. Continue this procedure until you have 12 in the dish. Reserve one cup sauce, cup cheese and 5 tablespoons onion. Mix the sour cream with reserved sauce. Pour over enchiladas, sprinkle with cheese, onion, green peppers and olives. Bake at 375 degrees F. for about 25 to 30 minutes, until tortillas are browned! Enjoy! Serves 6.

A two-time all-american forward at Texas Tech, Swoopes was the consensus 1993 national player of the year in women's college basketball. A gold medalist at Atlanta, she now plays for the Houston Comets of the WNBA.

Sheryl Swoopes

Hakeem Olajuwan

Rocket Linguine

8	ounces linguine
2	tablespoons olive oil
1/2	pound calamari, cleaned
1/4	pound medium shrimp, cooked, peeled and cut in half
2	cloves garlic, minced or pressed
8	roma tomatoes, peeled, seeded and cut into medium dice
2	tablespoons basil leaves cut into thin strips
	Salt and pepper to taste

Add linguine to salted boiling water and cook until al dente, 7 to 10 minutes.

While pasta is cooking, heat olive oil in a medium saute pan, over medium-high heat. Add calamari and cook 30 to 45 seconds. Add shrimp and cook, stirring, another 20 to 30 seconds. Add garlic and cook 10 to 15 seconds, stirring continually to keep from sticking to pan. Add tomatoes and basil, season with salt and pepper to taste. Cook until very hot throughout.

Drain cooked pasta, toss with seafood mixture and serve. Serves 2

The Admiral's Chicken Noodle Soup

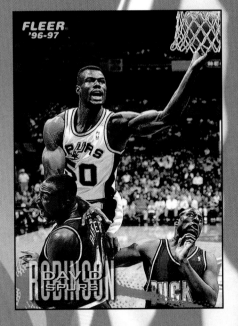

3	tablespoons extra virgin olive oil
1	cup diced onion
1	cup diced carrot
1	cup diced celery
1	teaspoon minced garlic
2	tablespoons white wine
1	gallon water plus 3 ounces chicken base or 1 gallon chicken stock or chicken broth
1	pound boneless chicken breasts
2	tablespoons chopped parsley] Salt and freshly ground black pepper to taste
12	ounces cooked fettucine, drained, in large pieces

● ●

Not only does this cure the common cold, but it keeps me going during the long, grueling NBA season. Put my recipe up against any other and compare. Move over grandma.

In medium saucepan, heat oil and add onions, carrots and celery. Stir about 5 minutes, until onions are translucent. Add garlic and stir. Add white wine and chicken stock. Add the chicken breasts, bring soup to a boil, and simmer until chicken is cooked through, about 5 minutes. Remove chicken from soup. When cool enough to handle, dice chicken, and return it to soup. Add the parsley and fettucine and season to taste with salt and pepper. Serves 6 to 8.

David Robinson

The Admiral has led the league in rebounding (13.0 in 1991), scoring (29.8 in 1994) and blocked shots (4.49 in 1992). He was named the NBA's MVP in 1995 and was a member of the Olympic teams in 1988, '92 and '96.

Stackhouse

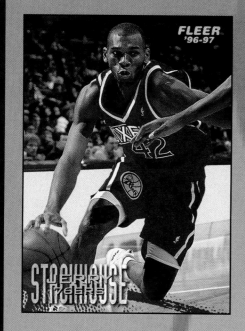

Takin' It To The Hole Crunchy Chicken Imperial

2	cups sour cream
1/4	cup fresh lemon juice
4	teaspoons Worcestershire sauce
2	teaspoons celery salt
2	teaspoons paprika
1	teaspoon salt
1	teaspoon black pepper
8	whole chicken breasts, split in half, boned and skinned, to make 16 chicken cutlets
1	16-ounce bag stuffing mix
3	tablespoons melted butter (optional)

Stack scored 27 points in his league debut and went on to win All-Rookie honors averaging 19.2 points per game in 1995-96 for the Philadelphia 76ers. He improved the next season by scoring 20.7 points per game.

Mix the sour cream, lemon juice, Worcestershire sauce, celery salt, paprika, salt and black pepper together in a bowl. Add the chicken cutlets and mix well. Put in a zip-lock bag and refrigerate overnight. When ready to cook, process stuffing mix in a blender or food processor until very finely ground. Dip each chicken piece in crumbs until completely coated. Arrange chicken pieces in single layer in a shallow baking dish and and preheat oven to 325 degrees F. Bake 1-1/4 hours, or until chicken is tender. If desired, brush with butter after it is done, but not if you are watching your weight. Serves 8 to 10.

Rim Rockin' Baked Orange Roughy with Garden Vegetables

1	pound orange roughy fillets
1	medium zucchini
1	carrot
1	red pepper
1	bunch scallions
1	clove garlic
5	fresh basil leaves
12	fresh Roma tomatoes
1/2	cup chicken broth
	Juice from 1 lemon
1	tablespoon butter or margarine
3	tablespoons fresh grated Parmesan cheese
	Blackened spice and black pepper to taste

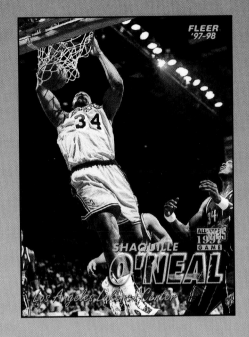

When I'm not on the court or working on the microphone, I love to get busy in the kitchen. This is one of my favorite healthy dishes to prepare and it's also good for you.

Preheat oven to 350 degrees F. Clean fillets well under cold water and place in a square baking dish. Slice zucchini into 1/4-inch rounds. Peel carrot and slice into thin circles. Seed pepper and dice into small squares. Chop scallions, garlic, and basil and slice tomatoes. Place vegetables atop the fillets then the scallions, garlic and basil. Pour the chicken broth and lemon juice over all. Place butter on top of the fillets and sprinkle with Parmesan cheese. Season with blackening spice and fresh ground pepper. Bake at 350 degrees F. for 10 to 12 minutes or until fish flakes away easily. Serves 3 to 4.

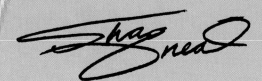

At 7'1" and 30_ lbs., Shaq ha_ proven to b_ nearly unstoppabl_ under the baske_ He has average_ 27.0 points an_ 12.5 rebounds pe_ game during h_ five-year caree_ with the Orland_ Magic and L_ Angeles Lakers

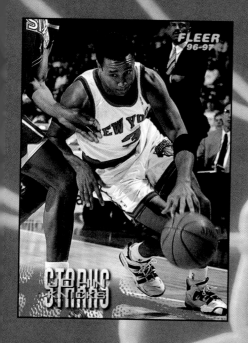

Three-Point Pasta

Sauce:

2	teaspoons extra virgin olive oil
1	cup chopped onion
2	cloves garlic
1	28-ounce can crushed tomatoes
1	6-ounce can tomato paste
1	tablespoon sugar
1	teaspoon salt
1-1/2	teaspoons oregano
1	tablespoon red pepper
1/2	cup white wine
1	bay leaf

Pasta:

1	pound shrimp
1	pound clams
1	pound scallops
2	teaspoons extra virgin olive oil
1	clove garlic, minced
1	pound thin spaghetti, cooked according to package directions and drained
	Grated Parmesan cheese to taste

• •

In a saucepan, heat olive oil, then add onion and garlic. Cook until garlic is slightly brown. Add remaining ingredients for sauce and simmer uncovered for 1-1/2 hours or until sauce is thick, stirring occasionally. Remove bay leaf.

While sauce is cooking, thoroughly clean shrimp, clams and scallops. Steam clams until they open. Simmer shrimp and scallops until tender (5 to 7 minutes). Heat olive oil in a skillet. Add garlic and saute about 1 minute. Add garlic and seafood to sauce. Simmer for a few minutes, until everything is heated through. Pour over hot pasta and serve with freshly grated Parmesan cheese. Serves 6.

#3

Championship Chocolate Cake

1   stick unsalted butter
1/4 cup cocoa
1/2 cup vegetable oil
1   cup water
2   cups granulated sugar
1/2 cup buttermilk
2   eggs, lightly beaten
1   teaspoon baking soda
1   teaspoon vanilla

FROSTING
1   stick (8 tablespoons)
    unsalted butter
1/2 cup milk
1/2 cup cocoa
8   ounces (about 2 cups)
    confectioners sugar
1   teaspoon vanilla
1/2 cup chopped walnuts

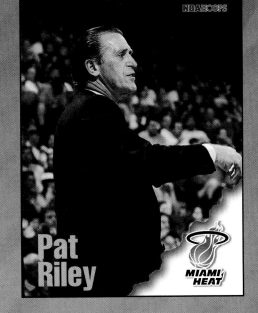

My last year as a basketball player was exciting as well as difficult. While my wife Chris and I were living in Phoenix, our best friend was our 65 year old neighbor. He always baked this cake for us which really helped to sweeten our lives. Every time we eat it, it brings back very fond memories.

To make the cake, grease a 9 x 13 - inch pan and set aside. Preheat oven to 350 degrees F. Whisk the butter, cocoa, oil and water together in a heavy saucepan until mixture comes to a boil. Mix the flour and sugar together in a large bowl. Pour the chocolate mixture over the flour mixture and stir well. Stir in the buttermilk, eggs, baking soda and vanilla. Pour batter into the prepared pan and bake at 350 degrees F. about 35 minutes, or until toothpick inserted in center of cake comes out clean.

For the frosting, bring the butter, milk and cocoa to a boil. Stir in the sugar, vanilla and nuts. Stir over low heat until mixture is thick and spreadable. Spread on cooled cake. Enjoy!

Riley has won more playoff games (145) than any other coach in NBA history. Stressing discipline, defense and the transition game, he led the Los Angeles Lakers to four championships between 1981 and '89.

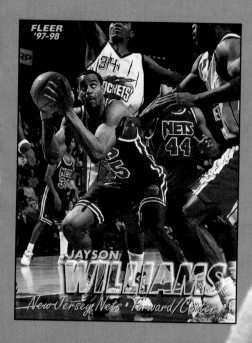

FLEER '97-98

JAYSON WILLIAMS
New Jersey Nets • Forward/Center

Off The Boards Caribbean Rice With Chicken

2-1/2	pounds chicken pieces
2	peppercorns (whole black pepper)
2	cloves garlic, peeled and minced
1	teaspoon dried oregano
4-1/2	teaspoons salt
2	teaspoons olive oil
1	teaspoon vinegar or fresh lime juice
1	tablespoon lard or vegetable oil
1	ounce salt pork, washed and diced
2	ounces lean cured ham
1	onion, peeled and chopped
1	green pepper, seeded and chopped
3	sweet chili peppers, seeded and chopped
1	tomato, chopped
6	fresh cilantro leaves
1	17-ounce can petit-pois peas
3	cups rice
1/2	teaspoon salt
10	olives, stuffed with pimentos
1	tablespoon capers
1/4	cup tomato sauce
2	tablespoons Achiote Coloring
1	4-ounce can or jar pimentos

Wash chicken and divide into small portions. Dry well and rub with a mixture of the peppercorns, garlic, oregano, salt, olive oil and vinegar. Marinate in refrigerator for several hours or overnight.

In a caldero or heavy kettle, heat lard and brown rapidly the salt pork and ham. Reduce heat to moderate, add chicken pieces and cook for 5 minutes. Reduce heat to low, and add the onion, green pepper, chili pepper, tomato and cilantro. Saute for 10 minutes, stirring occasionally.

Meanwhile, drain liquid from can of peas into a measuring cup and add enough water to measure 2 1/2 cups, if regular rice is used, and 3 cups if long-grain rice is used. Reserve peas. Heat liquid and reserve.

Add the salt, olives, capers, tomato sauce, achiote and rice to the kettle. Stir over moderate heat for 2 minutes. Stir in reserved hot liquid, mix well, and cook, uncovered, over moderate heat, for 5 minutes. With a fork, turn rice from bottom to top. Cover kettle and cook over low heat for 40 minutes. Halfway during this cooking period, turn rice over again. Add reserved peas, turn rice once more, cover, and cook for 15 minutes over low heat. Make sure there is enough liquid so rice doesn't burn. Add a little water if necessary. Spoon rice-chicken mixture onto a serving platter. Heat pimentos in their juice, drain and use for garnish. Serve at once. Serves 8.

CHECK IT OUT! A ROCKIN' COOKBOOK!

Recipes from over 100 of the world's most famous musical artists including: **Julio Iglesias** paella valencia, **Hootie and the Blowfish** peanut butter swirl bars, **Toni Braxton's** tofu cheesecake, **Travis Tritt's** hot and spicy chili, **Whitney Houston's** candied yams, **Sarah McLachlan's** chocolate chip banana bread, **Frank Sinatra's** Italian chicken, potato and onion dish, **Cher's** tuna pasta, **Coolio's** boneless turkey, **Madonna's** cherry torte and many more.

"A cacophony of taste"
— *People Magazine*

"Dolly Parton's version of floating island, is a very good version of the French classic custard and meringue dessert"
— *Suzanne Hamlin, New York Times*

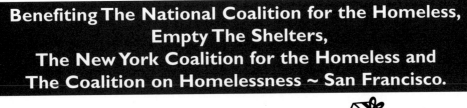

**Benefiting The National Coalition for the Homeless,
Empty The Shelters,
The New York Coalition for the Homeless and
The Coalition on Homelessness ~ San Francisco.**

A GREAT HOLIDAY GIFT!

Call 1~800~420~4209 to order

Global Liaisons, Incorporated/Publishers
P.O. Box 6049 NY, NY 10150

When the New Jersey Devils won the 1995 Stanley Cup, netminder Brodeur let in a paltry 1.67 goals per game. Stevens, a Devils defenseman, has made eight all-star appearances, including the last six in a row.

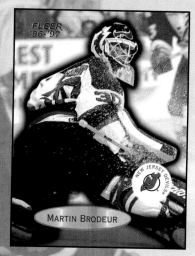

MARTIN BRODEUR

Shutout Sucre A La Creme

1	cup brown sugar
1	cup granulated sugar
1	cup heavy cream
1	teaspoon vanilla extract
1	tablespoon butter
1/2	cup ground nuts (optional)

Using a microwave-safe bowl, mix the brown sugar, granulated sugar and heavy cream together. Microwave on high for about 11 minutes. Mix twice during cooking. Add vanilla and butter and beat until thick. Stir in nuts if desired. Pour mixture into 8-inch square pan, and let cool in refrigerator, then cut in 2 x 2-inch squares. Makes 16 squares.

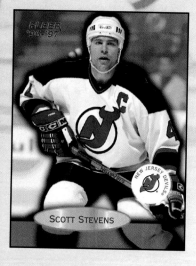

SCOTT STEVENS

Bone Crushin' Grilled Lamb Strips

5	pounds boneless butterflied leg of lamb, cut into strips
1	cup olive oil
	Juice of 3 lemons
	Salt and pepper to taste
4	bay leaves
1/2	cup crushed rosemary
2	teaspoons ginger
	Garlic powder to taste
	Mint leaves
	Mint jelly (optional)

Place lamb strips in shallow pan and pour 1/2 cup olive oil over top. Mix lemon juice, salt and pepper, bay leaves, rosemary, ginger, and garlic powder and pour half the mixture on the strips. Turn strips over, pour remaining olive oil over top, and add the remaining lemon juice mixture. Marinate 3 to 4 hours. Barbecue for 15 to 20 minutes over medium coals. Garnish with mint leaves and accompany with mint jelly if desired. Serves 10 to 12.

4	29-ounce cans, Hunt's tomato sauce
1	14.5 ounce cans Hunt's whole tomatoes, chopped
1	1-ounce can Hunt's tomato paste
1	medium Spanish onion
2	green bell peppers
3	garlic cloves
2	bay leaf
1	teaspoon sugar
3	tablespoons hot sauce
1/4	teaspoon salt
1/8	teaspoon pepper
1	dozen cleaned raw blue crabs
1	can fresh crab claw meat

In-the-Crease Crab Enchalaw

As a young boy growing up in Sault St. Marie, Canada, I watched my grandmother cook her homemade tomato sauce. She taught me how to cook this delicious sauce and most of all her secret . . . long slow cooking. When I moved to Florida and started up the first NHL (National Hockey League) franchise in the southeast, the Tampa Bay Lightning, I discovered Florida's incredible seafood, including my favorite blue crabs. With a little imagination I combined my grandmothers tomato sauce and blue crabs to create crab enchalaw. I hope you enjoy my recipe as well as my grandmother's as much as I do.

Chop green peppers, onions and garlic cloves. Using a large skillet, heat olive oil and mix in chopped peppers, onion and garlic, using salt and pepper for flavor, saute chopped mixture on medium heat, until tender, set aside.

In a large cooking pot, add tomato sauce, tomato paste, chopped whole tomatoes and hot sauce. Stir in pepper, onion and garlic mixture, sugar, bay leaf and 3 cleaned raw whole blue crabs. These 3 crabs only give the sauce flavor while cooking, and will be discarded later.

Cook sauce on low heat for approximately 6-8 hours or until sauce thickens. Stir occasionally. Long slow cooking makes the sauce thick and rich with flavor. Do not attempt to cut down on cooking time by increasing heat.

How to prepare the crabs for cooking: Buy fresh cleaned raw blue crabs.

Using kitchen scissors or a knife, cut off claws (2) and legs. Discard the crab legs. If you like you may cut the crab bodies in half to yield more pieces. Pre-crack the crab claws using a seafood cracker or a nut cracker. Place crab claws and bodies in the refrigerator until time to use.

Approximately 20 minutes before sauce has cooked completely, remove the 3 whole crabs and discard. Add crabs, stirring into the sauce the remaining prepared raw blue crab claws and bodies.

Cook sauce for 20 more minutes. Just before serving, stir in can fresh crab claw meat. Serve crab sauce and crab shells over your favorite cooked pasta. Sprinkle with your favorite grated cheese if desired. Don't forget to use small seafood forks to dislodge the crab meat from the crab shells while eating.

Freeze any remaining crab sauce in an airtight container. The crab sauce can be kept frozen for several months. Just defrost, heat and serve over fresh cooked pasta. Serves 8 to 10.

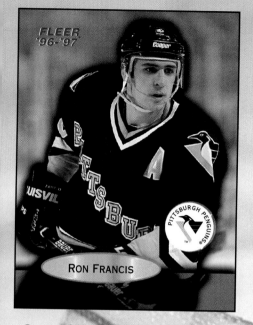

RON FRANCIS

Top Shelf Carrot Nut Cake

2	cups all-purpose flour
2	teaspoons baking powder
1	teaspoon baking soda
1	teaspoon salt
1	teaspoon cinnamon
2	cups sugar
1	cup corn oil
4	eggs
4	cups grated raw carrots
1	cup finely chopped walnuts

One of Ron's favorites and, of course, it's dessert!

Preheat oven to 325 degrees F. Oil and line the bottom of two 9-inch round layer cake pans with waxed paper and set aside. Sift together the flour, baking powder, baking soda, salt and cinnamon. Add the sugar gradually to oil. Beat well after each addition on high. Beat eggs until very light. Gradually beat eggs, a little at a time, into the oil/sugar mixture. Continue beating until mixture is smooth and fluffy. Gradually stir in the sifted dry ingredients until thoroughly combined. Add the carrots and nuts. Mix well. Pour into prepared pans and bake at 325 degrees F. for 60 to 65 minutes, or until layers are golden brown and the cake surface springs back when lightly touched.

Cool on a rack for 20 minutes before removing from pans. When completely cooled, spread icing (below) on top and sides. Makes 1 9-inch 2-layer cake.

Cream Cheese Icing

1	8-ounce package cream cheese
3	tablespoons corn oil
1/2	cup sifted confectioner sugar
1/2	teaspoon salt

Cream the cheese with a fork. Blend in corn oil. Gradually add the sugar and salt. Mix until smooth. Spread on cooled cake. Makes enough for 1 9-inch 2-layer cake. Enjoy!

Fresh Garden Salsa

3   medium onions
3   medium tomatoes
1/2 cup chopped cilantro
     Taco seasoning to taste
     Jalapenos to taste
     Salt and pepper to taste

• •

Chop up the onions and tomatoes (do the onions first so that
the tomatoes don't get too watery). Add the taco seasoning,
jalapenos, salt and pepper and cilantro to give it the final touch
of excellence. I also add different sauces to make it hotter
(the way I like it!)

Makes 2 cups Salsa.

*My wife bought me a chopper at a flea market in Palm Springs. I
started to make and experiment with my own sauce-never to buy it
out of a jar again! It was much healthier, fresher and the taste
was ten times better. Of course, now I've bought at least ten or
twelve of them and given them as gifts to all my friends and family.*

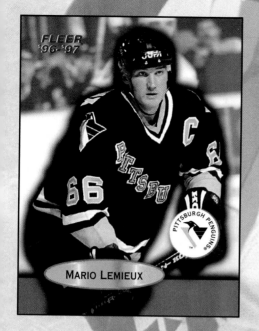

MARIO LEMIEUX

Super Mario's Magnificent Spimanti

1	pound Italian bread or pizza dough
	Garlic powder to taste
	Black pepper to taste
	Oregano to taste
	Crushed red pepper to taste
1	pound pepperoni
1	pound provolone cheese
1	pound prosciutto ham, sliced thin

Roll dough into a large, thin square. Sprinkle spices on dough. Layer pepperoni, provolone and prosciutto on dough, one layer at a time. Roll dough towards center from all sides to make a closed round loaf. Place on a baking sheet, and bake at 375 degrees F for 45 minutes. Serves 4 to 6.

Stick Handling
Chicken Paprikash

JAROMIR JAGR

2   pounds chicken pieces
1   tablespoon paprika
3   ounces margarine
1   medium onion, chopped
        Salt and pepper to taste
        Water (3 to 4 cups, depending on
        desired quantity of sauce)
16   ounces sour cream
1/2   cup flour

• •

Saute onion in margarine until tender. Add the paprika and chicken pieces. When chicken is browned, cover and continue to cook until the chicken is done. Add water as needed so chicken will not burn. Once meat is cooked, add 3 to 4 cups water. Bring to a boil. Mix flour into the sour cream. Stir very well. Add this mixture to the chicken and boiling water. Stir and simmer until the sauce has thickened. Add salt and pepper to taste.

Serve with buttered noodles or pasta. Serves 6.

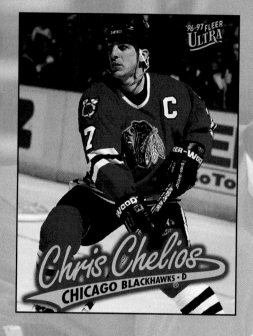

"Bone Jarring" Chili

1/2	cup olive oil
1	onion, chopped
1	zucchini, chopped
2	teaspoons chili powder
2	teaspoons ground cumin
1	teaspoon dried oregano
1	teaspoon paprika
2	pounds beef tenderloin, cut into inch cubes
1	28- ounce can plum tomatoes, with liquid
1	cup beef stock
1	tablespoon sugar
2	1-pound cans of red kidney beans, drained
	Salt and pepper to taste
1	cup non-fat sour cream
4	scallions, chopped

Heat 1/4 cup of the oil in a flameproof casserole dish. Add the onion, zucchini, chili powder, cumin, oregano and paprika. Cook over medium-low heat for 5 minutes. Add the remaining oil, and brown the meat over high heat, in batches if necessary.

Stir in the tomatoes, beef stock, and sugar. Simmer, uncovered, until the beef is tender, approximately 1-3/4 hours, covering the pot when the mixture becomes thick. Add kidney beans 15 minutes before beef is done. Season with salt and pepper. Serve with sour cream and scallions. This is also great with rice!
Serves 4

The Great One's Four Cup Chili

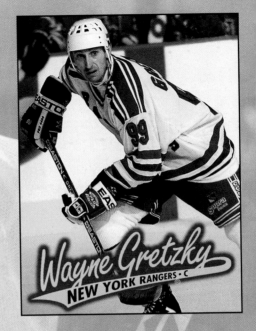

2	pounds ground beef
1	medium onion, diced
1	16 ounce can tomato paste
1	16 ounce can Mexican style stewed tomatoes
1	packet chili spices and seasonings
1	16 ounce can of Hunt's chili beans

Toppings:
Chopped onion
Grated cheddar cheese
Sour cream

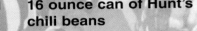

Lightly brown ground beef and drain off the juices. In a separate skillet, saute the onions in the juices. until tender. Drain onions and add to ground beef. Continue to cook on medium, adding tomatoes, paste, seasonings and beans, until thoroughly mixed and hot throughout. Top with chopped onion, grated cheese and sour cream. Serves 6.

I know my chili's good because the kids love to eat and sometimes wear it. It's one of my favorite recipes during the cold months of hockey season, especially after practice before my afternoon nap.

These three formed the heart of the Florida Panthers attack in 1996-97: Sheppard, a right wing, led the team with 60 points; Muller, a center, had 10 power play goals; Niedermayer, a center, had 40 points in 60 games.

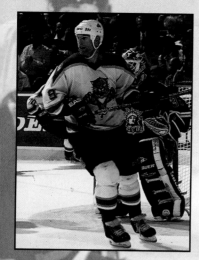

Hip-Check Tomato Fettucine with Snow Peas Alfredo

1/2	cup heavy cream
1	egg yolk, lightly beaten
1/4	cup freshly grated Parmesan cheese
1-1/2	tablespoons unsalted butter
	Coarse kosher salt and freshly ground black pepper to taste
1	pound tomato fettucine
1/4	pound snow peas, cleaned, trimmed and blanched 2 minutes in boiling water

In a heavy skillet or saute pan heat the cream to a simmer. Stir a bit of the hot cream into the egg yolk, then add the yolk to the cream. Do not boil or the egg will curdle. Over low heat, stir in the cheese and butter and season with salt and pepper. Cook the pasta in a large kettle of boiling lightly salted water until just tender. Drain. Gently toss the cooked pasta with the sauce until it coats the noodles. Add the snow peas and serve from a heated bowl or platter. Serves 4.

Red Light Chicken Broccoli Casserole

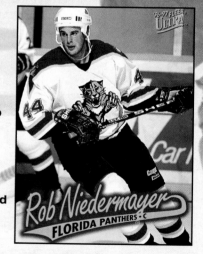

Rob Niedermayer
FLORIDA PANTHERS • C

3	large whole chicken breasts
2	10-ounce cans condensed chicken/mushroom soup
1/2	soup can milk
1/2	cup mayonnaise
8	ounces fresh sliced mushrooms
1	10-ounce package frozen broccoli, cooked according to package directions and drained
1/2	cup cracker crumbs

Poach the chicken breasts until tender, about 20 minutes. Let cool slightly, then discard skin and bones. Slice chicken into chunks or strips, as preferred, and set aside. Preheat the oven to 350 degrees F. and butter a casserole dish. Heat the soup, milk and mayonnaise in a saucepan. Add the mushroom and cook, stirring, until mushrooms are tender, about 2 minutes. Distribute the broccoli over the bottom of the buttered casserole dish. Top with the chicken and pour the sauce over all. Sprinkle the crumbs over the top and bake at 350 degrees F. for 20 minutes. Serve with rice. Serves 4.

Hattrick Porcupine Meatballs

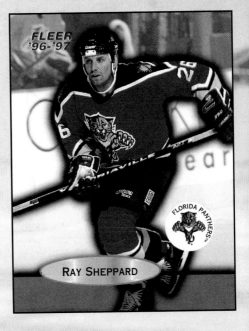

RAY SHEPPARD

1   pound lean ground beef
1   small onion, chopped
2   cups cooked rice
1   very small green pepper, seeded and chopped
1/4   teaspoon garlic salt or seasoned salt (optional)
     Salt and pepper to taste
1   10-ounce can condensed tomato soup
1   soup can water

Preheat oven to 350 degrees F. Combine all ingredients except soup and water. Shape into meatballs. Place in casserole. Pour the soup and water over all. Bake at 350 degrees F. for 1 hour. Serves 3 to 4.

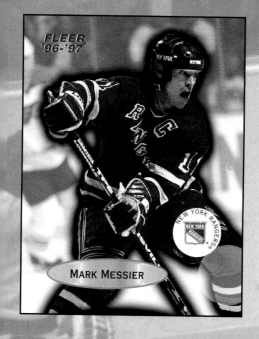

FLEER '96-'97

NEW YORK RANGERS

MARK MESSIER

Stanley Cup Spicy Sauce Over Sautéd Fish

1	tablespoon olive oil
1	tablespoon minced garlic
1	tablespoon peeled and minced fresh ginger
1	tablespoon soy sauce
1	teaspoon chili garlic paste (available in Asian markets)
1	cup fish or chicken stock
1	tablespoons cornstarch

Heat oil in small saucepan over medium heat for 2 minutes. Add garlic and cook, stirring, until dark golden in color. Add ginger and cook 1 minute more. Then add soy sauce and chili paste and stir. Mix cornstarch with 1 tablespoon of the stock. Add stock to sauce and bring just to a boil. Then add cornstarch mixture and cook, stirring until just thickened. Pour over freshly steamed fish and serve immediately.

Any fresh fish is great - Mark's pick is grouper. Serve on steamed rice, with extra sauce and fresh vegetables in season.

Serves 4 to 6

My favorite activity in the off season is fishing. When I am not playing hockey, my family and I are all eating fish 7 days a week, so, we need to get creative to spice up our choices. Here is one of our summertime favorites.

Leftwingers Robitaille and Graves combined for 109 points for the New York Rangers in the 1996-97 season. Graves scored 33 goals and 28 assists, while Robitaille had 24 goals and 24 assists.

Goal Scoring Healthy Turkey Chili

1	15-1/2 ounce can black beans	1	teaspoon cumin Chili powder to taste
1	15-1/2 ounce can red kidney or pinto beans	1/2	pound ground turkey, browned and well drained (optional)
1	15-1/2 ounce can white beans	1/2	cup shredded cheddar cheese (optional)
2	cups frozen corn kernels (or 1 16 ounce can corn, drained)	1/4	cup sour cream (optional) Sliced jalapeno peppers (optional)
2	16 ounce cans stewed tomatoes (preferably Mexican style)		
2	small cans chopped green chilies		

Combine the beans, corn, tomatoes, chilies, cumin, chili powder and turkey in a large pot. Cook until heated through, about 15 minutes. Serve topped with shredded cheddar cheese, jalapeno peppers, and/or sour cream, and cooked rice. Serves 4 to 6.

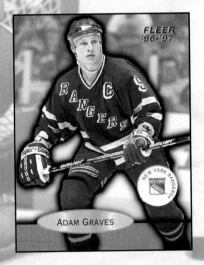

ADAM GRAVES

FLEER '96-'97

Power Forward Fat Free Spinach Dip

1	10 ounce package frozen chopped spinach, boiled or microwaved according to package directions
1	cup fat free sour cream
1	cup fat free mayonnaise
1	package dried vegetable soup mix
2	scallions, chopped
1	teaspoon garlic powder
1	teaspoon seasoned salt

Drain and squeeze spinach well and set aside. Combine remaining ingredients in mixing bowl. Stir in drained spinach. Refrigerate 2 hours before serving. Makes about 4 cups. A festive way of serving this dip is to take a round loaf of pumpernickel bread. Cut a circle out of the top loaf and remove. Gently pull bread from inside to be later used to dip. When ready to serve, pour dip into hollowed out bread and serve.

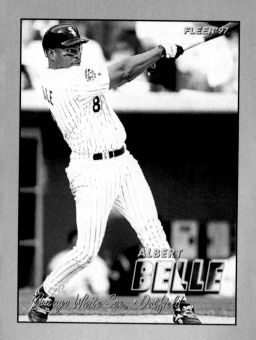

Julie's Jambalaya

1-1/2 pounds chicken
2 tablespoons vegetable oil
1 green pepper, seeded and chopped
1 red pepper, seeded and chopped
1 small yellow onion, chopped
2 scallions, chopped
3-1/2 cups canned chicken broth
1 teaspoon Tabasco sauce
1/4 cup Worcestershire sauce
1 tablespoon red (Cajun) pepper
1 teaspoon paprika
2 cups uncooked converted rice

• •

Bake chicken in a shallow baking pan at 350 degrees F. for 40 minutes. Remove from oven and set aside. Place oil in a medium frying pan. Sauté yellow onion, green pepper, red pepper and scallions until tender. Bring the chicken broth to a boil in a 2-quart stockpot. Add vegetables. Cover and simmer over low heat for 15 minutes. While the broth and vegetables simmer, cut the baked chicken into bite-sized pieces. Discard any bones. Bring the chicken broth and vegetables back to a boil. Add the chicken, Tabasco sauce, Worcestershire sauce, red pepper, black pepper, and paprika. Cover and simmer over low heat for 15 minutes. Bring back to a final boil and add rice. Cover and simmer over low heat for 30 minutes. Serve with garden salad and cornbread muffins.

Makes 4 servings (or one and a half servings for a 210-pound professional athlete.)

Hint: To save time, bake chicken the day before preparing main dish or use 1 1/2 cups leftover roast chicken.

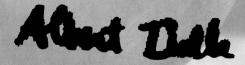

Fish:

1	clove garlic, crushed
4	7-ounce swordfish steaks
1	tablespoon extra virgin olive oil
	Salt and pepper to taste

Combine above ingredients and marinate overnight in refrigerator. Preheat grill and cook swordfish until done. To serve, spread some White Bean Green Sauce (below) on plate. Place a swordfish steak on top of sauce, and top fish with a scoop of Grilled Pepper Relish (below). Garnish with cilantro leaves if desired, and serve with rice. Serves 4.

White Bean Green Sauce:

3/4	cup small dried white beans
3	cups chicken broth
1	cup fresh cilantro leaves
1/2	cup fresh parsley leaves
	White pepper to taste

Grand Slam Grilled Swordfish with Grilled Pepper Roasted Garlic Relish

Soak dry beans overnight in water. Drain and place beans in pot. Cover and simmer beans in chicken broth until soft. Drain remaining liquid and reserve one cup to adjust consistency of sauce. Place beans in blender with parsley and cilantro. Add half of reserved liquid and blend on high speed until beans are thoroughly pureed. Add remaining liquid until desired consistency is reached. Makes about 2 cups.

Grilled Pepper Relish:

1	red pepper
1	yellow pepper
3	cloves roasted garlic
2	tablespoons balsamic vinegar
1	tablespoon extra virgin olive oil
1	tablespoon fresh cilantro leaves
1	twist white pepper
	Dash salt

Place whole peppers on high grill. Burn skin until black, let cool, then peel off skin and remove seeds. Julienne peppers and toss gently with remaining ingredients. Marinate overnight. Makes about 1 cup.

The versatile Bonilla has been named an all-star as a first baseman, third baseman and outfielder. In 1996 he hit a major league record 17 sacrifice flies and had 116 RBI for the Baltimore Orioles.

Dave Cone

Winning Spinach Noodle Casserole

8	ounces broad egg noodles
3	tablespoons butter
2	tablespoons flour
1	cup skim milk, scalded
1/2	teaspoon salt
1/2	teaspoon paprika
1/4	teaspoon black pepper
1/8	teaspoon nutmeg
2	10-ounce packages frozen spinach, cooked and well drained
1/2	pound Swiss cheese, shredded

Cone won the 1994 Cy Young Award by going 16-5 with a 2.94 ERA for the Kansas City Royals. He also struck out 19 batters in a game while with the New York Mets. Cone has won World Series rings with the New York Yankees and Toronto Blue Jays. In 1997, David struck out his 2000th batter.

Preheat oven to 400 degrees F. Cook noodles according to package directions, drain and rinse. In saucepan, melt butter, stir in flour and cook for one minute while stirring. Gradually add milk and bring to a boil. Cook until thickened, stirring constantly. Add seasonings and spinach. Stir and remove from heat. In a greased baking dish, arrange half of the noodles and sprinkle with half of the cheese. Spoon spinach mixture over cheese. Add another layer of noodles and sprinkle with the rest of the cheese. Cover and bake at 400 degrees F. for 15 minutes. Remove cover and bake for an additional 15 minutes more. Serves 4.

Caminiti

4   egg whites
       Pinch salt
1/4   teaspoon cream of tartar
1   cup sugar
6   ounces semisweet
       chocolate morsels
6   tablespoons water
1   pint heavy cream
1/3   cup sugar
1-2   pints fresh strawberries

Hot Corner Strawberry Cake

• • • • • • • • • • • • • • • • • • • •

Beat egg whites, salt and cream of tartar until stiff and glossy. Gradually beat in 1 cup sugar. Beat until very stiff. Make three 8-inch circles out of parchment paper. Place on baking sheet and spread the meringue evenly on the circles. It should be about 1/4 inch thick. Bake for 25 minutes in a preheated 250 degree F. oven. Meringue should be slightly golden. Remove from oven and peel the paper carefully off the back. Put on racks to cool and dry.

For the chocolate layer, bring water to boil and put chocolate morsels into pan. Cover and set aside. The chocolate will melt while doing the next step. Stir to mix. Stiffly whip cream, gradually adding sugar. Beat until very stiff. Slice strawberries (save some to decorate cake).

To assemble, put a meringue layer on a serving plate. Carefully spread a layer of melted chocolate, using half the chocolate. Spread a half-inch layer of whipped cream and top with half the sliced strawberries. Repeat with second meringue, chocolate, whipped cream and strawberries. Place last meringue on top. Frost with remaining whipped cream (cover sides and top). Decorate with extra strawberries or chocolate curls. Refrigerate for at least two hours. Makes an 8-inch cake.

In 1996, Caminiti hit .326 with 40 home runs and 130 RBI to earn the National League MVP award. His RBI total equaled Mickey Mantle's record for switch-hitters and he is the first player to hit home runs from both sides of the plate three times in one season.

Jeter

Double-Play Chicken Parmesan

6	skinless boneless chicken breast halves
1/3	cup flour
2	egg whites, slightly beaten
1	cup Italian bread crumbs
1	tablespoon grated Parmesan cheese
1/4	cup red onion, chopped
1	clove garlic
2	cups prepared spaghetti sauce
6	thin slices mozzarella cheese

The 1996 American League Rookie of the Year batted .314 and had 78 RBI for the world champion New York Yankees. In the post-season, the rookie shortstop hit .361 and scored 12 runs in 15 games.

Dredge chicken with flour. Dip in egg whites until coated. Combine bread crumbs and Parmesan cheese. Roll chicken in bread crumb mixture until completely covered. In a frying pan, heat oil. Sauté onion and garlic for about 2 minutes. Add chicken and cook about 5 to 6 minutes per side. Transfer to a baking pan. Top with favorite spaghetti sauce and one thin slice of mozzarella cheese. Bake in 350 degree F. oven for 20 minutes or until tender. Serves 6.

Justice

Over-the-Fence Fruit Cocktail Cake

DAVID JUSTICE
Cleveland Indians • Outfield

Cake:
2   cups flour
1-1/2 cups sugar
1   stick butter
2   eggs, beaten
2   teaspoons baking soda
1   teaspoon vanilla
     Pinch Salt
1   20-ounce can
     fruit cocktail with juice

Frosting:
1   stick butter
1/2   cup canned evaporated milk
1   teaspoon vanilla
1   cup sugar
1/4   cup chopped walnuts or other nuts
1   cup shredded coconut

• •

Preheat oven to 350 degrees F. Mix all cake ingredients and pour into greased 9x13-inch pan. Bake 30 to 35 minutes. Remove to cool on a rack. Stir Frosting ingredients in a saucepan to a rolling boil. Let cool then spread over cake. Makes 1 9x13-inch cake; 2 cups frosting.

The 1990 National League Rookie of the Year can hit for power (40 home runs and 120 RBI in '93) and average (.313 in '94). Justice, now a Cleveland Indian, also had four home runs and 14 RBI in 19 World Series games with the Atlanta Braves.

Piazza

Karros

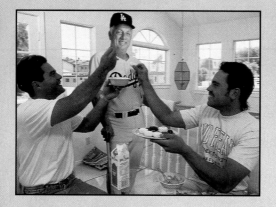

Batting Practice Mini Pizza

Former Rookies-of-the-year have to stick together you know. Life is more than a bowl of cereal and we love to get to work in the kitchen before and after running the bases. Tommy always stressed the importance of good eating and we concur.

1	13 ounce can refrigerated pizza dough
2	tablespoons olive oil
2	cups chopped onions
1	pound lean ground beef
4	tablespoons tomato paste
1	teaspoon sugar
1	teaspoon ground cumin
1	teaspoon paprika
1/2	teaspoon cayenne pepper
2	cups mozzarella cheese, grated
	Dash salt

Divide dough into 4 equal pieces and roll out to 1/4 inch thick. Heat oil in frying pan, add onions and cook for about 5 minutes. Add the beef, tomato paste, sugar, cumin, paprika, cayenne pepper and dash of salt. Cook for 5 more minutes, remove from heat. Spoon the beef mixture onto the pizza rounds, add cheese to each one. Put on baking sheet and bake the pizzas for about 15 minutes at 450°.

• •

White Sauce:

3	cups chicken stock (reserved from cooking chicken)
2-1/2	tablespoons cornstarch
1	cup strained unflavored yogurt (at room temperature)
2	tablespoons dry white wine
3	tablespoons capers
1	tablespoon red wine vinegar
1	tablespoon dried basil
1	tablespoon minced parsley
	Salt and pepper to taste

Chicken Scallopini with White Sauce

Spaghetti:

1 to 3	1/2 pound chicken
1	small onion, chopped
4	stalks celery, chopped
2	tablespoons chopped parsley
	Steamed vegetables (optional)
1	pound cooked spaghetti

Rinse the chicken, put in a large pot and cover with cold water. Add the onion, celery and parsley, bring to a boil, reduce heat, and cook for 1 hour and 20 minutes. Drain, reserving stock. When chicken is cool enough to handle, discard all skin, fat and bones. Break the meat into 3-inch pieces. If you would like to serve vegetables with this dish, steam your favorites (carrots, peas, mushrooms, etc.). Make white sauce (below) while chicken is cooling. To serve, place cooked spaghetti on a platter. Arrange chicken pieces over spaghetti, and pour white sauce over chicken. Garnish with steamed vegetables. Serve hot and enjoy. Serves 4.

To make sauce, pour chicken stock into medium saucepan. Bring to a boil, then reduce heat to simmer, and cook for 10 minutes. Remove from heat, stir in cornstarch, and boil for 30 seconds, stirring continuously, until thickened. Remove from heat and let cool. In a small bowl, gently stir yogurt, making sure all lumps are dissolved. Stir yogurt into the cooled sauce. Slowly reheat the sauce on a low flame and add the wine, capers, vinegar, basil, parsley, and salt and pepper to taste. Use with chicken and spaghetti above. Makes 2-1/2 cups sauce.

Mike Piazza—The 1993 rookie of the year, Piazza has been the National League's All-Star catcher since his first full season in the majors. He has averaged more than 100 RBI and 30 home runs per season for his career with the Los Angeles Dodgers.

Eric Karros— After being named NL Rookie of the Year in 1992, Karros has continued to produce for the Los Angeles Dodgers. The first baseman has averaged more than 20 home runs and 85 RBI per season for his career.

Pinstripe Chicken Fried Steak with Cream Gravy

1	cup all-purpose flour
1	teaspoon salt
1	teaspoon white pepper
1	teaspoon garlic powder
3	whole eggs, beaten
1	clove garlic, chopped fine
1	tablespoon fresh chopped parsley
4	cups vegetable oil
2	4-ounce pieces filet mignon, pounded thin

• •

Combine in one bowl, flour, salt, pepper and garlic powder.

In another bowl mix eggs, chopped garlic and parsley. Heat oil in a 10 inch skillet. Place each piece of meat in flour mixture, then in egg mixture, then back in flour mixture. Place in skillet.

Cook about 3 minutes, flip over. Cook about 3 more minutes till golden brown. Place on paper towel to remove some of the oil. Place each steak on plate. Top with gravy. Serve with mashed potatoes and vegetables of your choice.

Garnish with a sprig of parsley. Serves 2

This recipe was submitted by the Mantle family in memory of one the greatest players to ever step on the baseball diamond. This dish was Mick's favorite from his days growing up in Oklahoma to the bright lights of Yankee Stadium and memorable autumn afternoons.

The most powerful switch-hitter in baseball history, Mantle belted 536 home runs and 1,509 RBI. He won the Triple Crown in 1956 with 52 home runs, 130 RBI and a .353 average. Baseball lost a legend when Mantle died of cancer.

• •

CREAM GRAVY:

3	tablespoons butter
3	tablespoons flour
2-1/2	cups heavy cream or milk
	Salt and white pepper to taste

Heat butter until it sizzles. Add flour. Cook, stirring constantly, about 1 minute. Add cream, salt and pepper. Bring to a boil. Simmer until thickened, about 3 minutes. Makes 2-1/2 cups.

Mickey Mantle

Jack McDowell

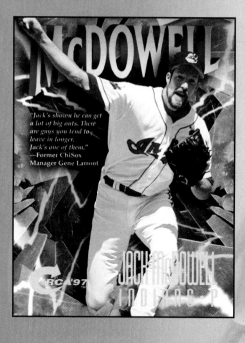

Black Jack's Toffee Bars

1	cup butter (softened)
1	cup packed light brown sugar
1	teaspoon vanilla
2	cups sifted all-purpose flour
1	6-ounce package semi-sweet chocolate chips
1	cup chopped walnuts

Cream the butter, sugar and vanilla. Add the flour and mix well. Stir in the chocolate chips and walnuts. Press into an ungreased 13" x 9" pan. Cook at 350° for 20 minutes. Cut while warm, cool completely before removing. Makes 12 to16 bars.

McDowell won the American League Cy Young Award in 1993 when he went 22-10 with a 3.37 ERA and a league-leading four shutouts. A workhorse, McDowell has led the league in complete games three times and has more than 65 in his ten-year career.

Favorite Zucchini Casserole

1	medium zucchini, cut in 1/4-slices
1	medium summer squash, cut in 1/4-slices
2	large tomatoes, cut in 1/4-slices
2	small onions, thinly sliced
1-1/2	cups unseasoned croutons
1/2	cup grated cheddar cheese

In your casserole dish, layer the ingredients in the following order: zucchini, 1/2 of the tomatoes, onion, croutons, salt and minimal pepper, summer squash, and the rest of the tomatoes.

Cover and bake in a preheated 375° oven for one hour. Remove from oven and add grated cheese to the top. Return to the oven, uncovered, 10 to 15 minutes. Serves 4 to 6.

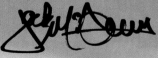

Palmeiro

R.B.I. Wash Dry Cake

1   box yellow cake mix
1   stick soft butter
1   egg
8   ounces cream cheese
2   eggs (additional)
1   box confectioner's sugar
1   teaspoon vanilla

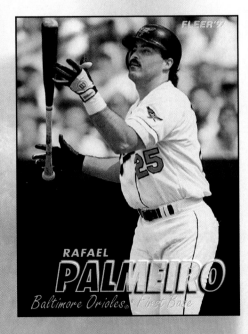

RAFAEL
PALMEIRO
Baltimore Orioles First Base

• •

Combine cake mix, butter and egg and mix well. Spread in 9 x 13-inch pan.

Mix cream cheese, eggs, sugar, and vanilla. Pour this over the batter in pan. Bake for 40 minutes in a 325° oven.

Once cool, cut in squares. Serves 8 to 10.

Palmeiro is best known for his production at the plate with a .298 career average and more than 250 home runs in his 12 year career. However, he has also led American League first basemen in assists five times.

75

Ripken

My mom, Vi Ripken, never met a potato she didn't like, and these dishes became staples in our family. My kids prefer hamburgers and hot dogs, but I didn't become Baseball's All-Time ironman without mom's hearty potato recipes. Hope you enjoy them!

Ironman Potato Casserole

8	ounces cream cheese
2	pounds frozen hash browns with green peppers and onions, slightly thawed (if you can only find plain hash browns, use that and add 1/2 cup sautéd onions and 1/2 cup sautéd green peppers)
1	10-ounce can cream of chicken soup
1	soup can (about 1-1/4 cups milk)
4	slices American cheese
3	cups crushed corn flakes
1-1/2	sticks margarine, melted

● ●

Preheat oven to 350 degrees F. Crumble the cream cheese and add to potatoes, onion and green peppers in an ovenproof casserole dish. Add soup and milk to mixture and blend. Cover the top with slices of American cheese. Top the cheese with crushed corn flakes. Pour melted margarine over the entire mixture and bake at 350 degrees F. for 1 hour. Serves 4 to 6.

World Series German Potato Salad

6	medium potatoes
4	slices bacon, cooked, drained and diced
1	small to medium cucumber, peeled and diced
1	small onion
3	tablespoons oil
3	tablespoons vinegar
	Beef bouillon cube dissolved in 1/2 cup water
	Parsley for garnish (optional)

Cut potatoes in slices or chunks and boil until tender. Drain well and add bacon, cucumber and onion. Add vinegar and oil; blend. Add bouillon mixture last. Serve warm or at room temperature, garnished with parsley if desired. Serves 4 to 6.

Ripken hasn't just played in more consecutive games than any other major leaguer, he's played them exceptionally well: The 14-time all-star has hit more home runs (345) than any shortstop in major league history.

1   pound jumbo lump
    crabmeat
8   ounces sour cream
16 ounces cream cheese
1/2 teaspoon dry mustard
    (or more to taste)
1 to 2 tablespoons
    Worcestershire sauce,
    to taste
2   tablespoons lemon juice
1   tablespoon Hellman's
    mayonnaise
1/2 cup grated cheddar cheese

Gold Glove
Maryland Crab Dip

*My daughter and my wife have
served this often and I love it.*

Mix everything together in large bowl, except 1/4 cup of
cheddar cheese, carefully folding in lumps of crabmeat.

Sprinkle remaining 1/4 cup cheddar on top and bake at
325 degrees F. for approximately 45 minutes. Serve with
crackers. Makes about 4 cups.

The greatest
fielding third
baseman in history;
Robinson won 16
consecutive gold
gloves during his
23 seasons with
the Baltimore
Orioles. He also
was named an
all-star 15 times
and hit 268
home runs.

Rusty Staub

A six-time all-star, Staub had 2,716 hits, 292 home runs and 1,466 RBI in his 23 major-league seasons as a catcher and outfielder. He hit .423 with six RBI for the New York Mets in the 1973 World Series.

Pinch Hit Red Snapper with Mushrooms

Sauce:
1/2 stick butter
6 chopped garlic cloves
1 teaspoon chopped fresh thyme
2 tablespoons chopped fresh basil
1/2 pound sliced mushrooms
6 shakes Worcestershire sauce
3 shakes Tabasco sauce
Salt and pepper to taste

• •

In a saute pan, melt butter and add garlic. Saute until translucent. Add basil and thyme and combine. Add mushrooms and saute until mushrooms soften. Stir in Worcestershire and Tabasco sauces and salt and pepper to taste. Remove from heat.

Fish:
2 6-ounce red snapper fillets
2 teaspoons balsamic vinegar
2 ounces thinly sliced butter

• •

Place red snapper on baking sheet. Press vinegar into filets gently with a fork and dot the fillets with the butter. Place into preheated 400 degree F. oven for approximately 8 minutes. Remove from oven and place fillets in a saute pan. Put mushroom sauce over fillets and saute for over 2 to 3 minutes to heat through. Remove fillets to platter and spoon mushrooms and sauce over all. Serves 2.

2 to 4 pounds beef tenderloin
1 cup Grand Marnier
1 cup barbecue sauce
2 teaspoons minced garlic
2 teaspoon minced onion
Salt and pepper to taste

"Well-Managed" Beef Grand Marnier

15

Place tenderloin in glass or loaf pan. Split middle slightly. Pour Grand Marnier and barbecue sauce over tenderloin. Season with garlic and onion. Add salt and pepper. Marinate in refrigerator four to six hours or longer if desired. Prepare coals on grill. Place loaf pan with tenderloin on grill. Cover and cook 45 minutes to one hour. Can be cooked in the oven but has a better barbecue flavor on the grill. Slice and serve. Serves 6 to 10.

Joe Torre

30

After playing for 18 years and managing for 14 years in the National League, Torre finally won a World Series ring in his first American League season while managing the New York Yankees in 1996. He appeared in eight all-star games as a player.

Frank Thomas

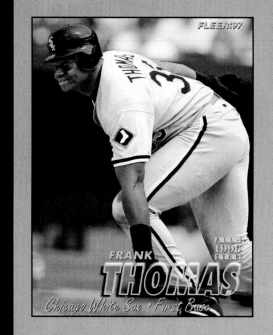

FRANK THOMAS
Chicago White Sox • First Base

Big Hurt's Power Pasta

2   16-ounce cans Italian
      plum tomatoes
1   large clove garlic, minced
6   tablespoons butter
'1/2 teaspoon lime juice (optional)
3   large leaves fresh basil, chopped
      Salt and pepper to taste
1   pound pasta (tortellini is Frank's
      favorite), cooked according to
      package directions and drained

The Big Hurt has averaged more than 35 home runs and nearly 120 RBI in his seven full seasons with the Chicago White Sox. His numbers would be even bigger if pitchers would throw to him: Thomas has led the league in walks four times.

Drain both cans of tomatoes, reserving the liquid from one can. Place tomatoes in food processor and chop coarsely. In a large pan, sauté minced garlic in two tablespoons butter until soft. Add reserved liquid from tomatoes and the chopped tomatoes. Boil down for 10 minutes. Add remaining butter, lime juice and chopped basil leaves. Simmer uncovered to desired consistency. Add salt and pepper to taste. Pour over your favorite pasta. Serves 4.

Green Monster Herbed Turkey Burger

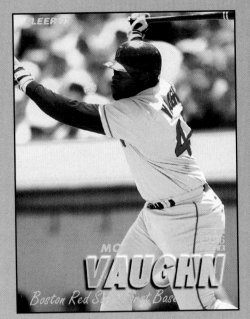

1	pound ground turkey
1/2	cup fresh whole wheat bread crumbs
4	green onions, chopped
3	tablespoons chopped fresh dill or 1 tablespoon dried dillweed
1	tablespoons Dijon mustard
2	egg white, beaten to blend
1/2	teaspoon salt
1/2	teaspoon ground pepper
	Nonstick vegetable oil spray
4	poppy seed kaiser rolls or buns, split
4	lettuce leaves
4	large tomato slices

Prepare barbecue to a medium-high heat. Combine turkey, bread crumbs, green onions, dill, mustard, egg white, salt and pepper in large bowl. Using hands, mix thoroughly. Shape turkey mixture into 4 patties, about 1/2 inch thick.

Spray grill track generously with vegetable oil spray. Grill turkey burgers until white in center but still juicy, about 6 minutes per side.

Place rolls, cut side down, at edge of grill and toast lightly, about 2 minutes. Transfer rolls to plates. Spread bottom half of each roll with Dijon mustard. Top with lettuce leaf, burgers, tomato slice and top of roll and serve. Serves 4.

Grandma's Ninth Inning Chicken Spaghetti

Low fat/fat free ingredients substitute well

6	boneless skinless chicken breasts
8	ounces spaghetti
2	tablespoons butter or margarine
1	medium onion
3	large celery stalks
1	10-ounce can diced tomatoes with green chilies
1	10-ounce can condensed cream of celery soup
2	10-ounce cans condensed cream of chicken soup
1/2	pound Velveeta cheese, cubed
	Salt and pepper to taste

• •

In ten cups of water, poach chicken breasts until tender. Remove chicken from broth and set aside. Cook spaghetti in broth until tender, stirring occasionally to prevent sticking. While spaghetti is cooking, cube chicken into small pieces.

Chop onion and celery and saute together in the butter. Set aside. Remove spaghetti and broth from heat but do not drain. Add the tomatoes with green chilies, the chicken and celery soups, the reserved onions and celery, the cubed Velveeta and the cubed chicken. Stir gently over low heat and warm through. Add salt and pepper to taste if desired. This freezes well too. Serves 10 to 12.

EVERY DAY,
NONPROFIT GROUPS
HELP PEOPLE
RUN, LAUGH, DANCE,
FEEL, SEE AND
MAKE LIFE BETTER.

WE'RE PROUD
TO PLAY A PART.

What makes a city great is the involvement of its people and the good work they do. Whether it's donating time to a

local charity, contributing to a museum or helping to organize a neighborhood festival. We're pleased to play a part in

charitable and community events in the cities we serve across the United States. And we support the thousands of local

American employees who give what time and effort they can right in their hometown.

AmericanAirlines®
American Eagle®

To find out more about American on the Internet, visit our web site at http://www.americanair.com
American Airlines and American Eagle are registered trademarks of American Airlines, Inc. American Eagle is American's regional airline associate.

Andre Agassi

Penne Arrabiate

2	fresh tomatoes, diced
3	cloves fresh garlic, diced
2	tablespoons olive oil
8	leaves of fresh basil, diced
4	ounces fresh Buffalo mozzarella
2	teaspoons grated parmesan cheese
1	teaspoon crushed red pepper
	Pinch of salt and pepper
1	tablespoon butter
1	pound penne rigata

Cook pasta in boiling salted water. Saute garlic and oil on medium high heat. Before the garlic turns brown, add the diced tomatoes, basil, red pepper, salt, pepper and butter. Continue cooking for 2-3 minutes at a low heat. If sauce thickens add a tablespoon of water from the cooking pasta.

Drain pasta and add to tomato sauce, gently tossing over medium heat. Add fresh mozzarella, toss and serve. Serves 2

4 cups cooked chicken chunks
1 cup pineapple chunks
1 cup celery
1/2 cup scallions
1/4 cup dry-roasted unsalted peanuts
1/2 teaspoon salt
2 tablespoons chutney
2 tablespoons lemon juice
1/2 lemon rind grated
1/2 teaspoon curry powder
2/3 cup mayonnaise

Center Court Healthy Chicken Salad

If possible, use fresh pineapple and low-fat low-cholesterol mayonnaise

Toss all the ingredients in a large mixing bowl. Serves 4.

I have always been health conscious and tried to teach my kids the same. My friends know me for my healthy chicken salad along with my baseline rallies and backhand. It's great for lunch on warm afternoons.

Chris Evert

Wimbledon Pesto

1	cup olive oil
2	cloves garlic
1/2	cup fresh basil leaves
1	teaspoon salt
1/4	teaspoon pepper
2	tablespoons pine nuts
1	cup parsley leaves
1	cup grated Parmesan cheese

Mix olive oil, garlic and basil in a blender or food processor until well chopped. Let sit for at least 15 minutes. Add salt, pepper and pine nuts and pulse until mixed. Add parsley and pulse until thoroughly mixed. Remove from machine and place in a medium bowl. Fold in Parmesan cheese to desired texture and flavor. Makes 2 cups.

Known as much for their on-court antics and their candor in the announcing booth as for their tennis prowess, their 1993 French Open doubles title attests that Luke and Murphy are a tough team to beat.

Fishing Scones with Raisins

Scones are found all over the British Isles. If you are serious about catching fish, take the time to mix the prescribed ingredients and then work with your tackle while your scones are baking on the day before the fishing trip

2	tablespoons butter
3	cups fine whole-wheat flour
2	teaspoons baking powder
1/4	cup light brown sugar
1/2	cup golden raisins
1	cup of sliced almonds
1	large egg, beaten
2/3	cup milk

• •

Preheat oven to 425 F and lightly grease a large baking sheet. Blend the butter, flour and baking powder, then stir in the sugar, raisins, and almonds. Make a hole in the center of the ingredients and pour in the beaten egg. Mix to a soft dough with the milk.

Knead the dough on a lightly floured surface until smooth, then roll out until half an inch thick. Cut out with a two (2) inch cutter and place the fishing scones on the prepared baking sheet.

Bake for 10 minutes in the preheated oven, then cool on a wire rack before packing for your fishing trip. Makes about 12.

Warning: Do not share with fresh water fish!

Kick Butt Borscht

5	fresh beet heads, boiled until tender and cooled
1	medium cucumber
5	scallions
1	sprig of green dill
1	cup sour cream
1	cup of buttermilk
1/2	half cup vinegar
7	cups cold water
Salt and pepper to taste	
Hot boiled potatoes (optional)	

Shred beets in a food Processor. Chop cucumber and scallions very fine, mince dill leaves. Whip sour cream and buttermilk together. Mix the beets, cucumber, onion and dill with the sour cream mixture, then add the vinegar, water and salt and pepper to taste. Serve hot or cold with hot boiled potatoes if desired.

Monica

8	ripe plum tomatoes or
1	16-ounce can tomatoes, drained
1	medium onion, chopped
1	tablespoon olive oil
2	cloves garlic, crushed
1	pinch ground red pepper
1	tablespoon chopped fresh basil or 1 teaspoon dried basil
2	cups skim or 1% milk
	Salt and freshly ground pepper to taste
	Fresh basil leaves for garnish (optional)

Seles, the winner of nine Grand Slam singles titles (four Australian Opens, three French Opens and two U.S. Opens), bravely came back to tennis in 1995 nearly two years after a deranged fan stabbed her courtside.

In a large pot of boiling water, blanch the ripe tomatoes for 10 seconds. Transfer to colander; cool slightly. Peel off skin. Cut tomatoes in half; remove seeds and chop. (Or, seed and chop canned tomatoes.) In a medium saucepan, cook the onion in olive oil over medium heat, stirring frequently, until onion is golden brown, about 4 minutes. Add the garlic and cook 1 minute longer. Add the chopped tomatoes and cook an additional 10 minutes.) Spoon three fourths of the mixture into food processor or blender container and puree until smooth.

Return mixture to saucepan. Add the red pepper, basil and milk to the soup. Heat through but do not boil. Season to taste with salt and pepper. Divide the soup into two warm bowls and serve immediately. Garnish with fresh basil leaves, if desired. Yields 4 cups. Serves 2.

Monica Seles

1 tablespoon olive oil
1 small onion, finely chopped
2 chilies, finely chopped
1 teaspoon dried basil or
2 teaspoon fresh basil leaves
1 16-ounce can tomatoes
1 tablespoon tomato paste
2 cups penne pasta, cooked
   according to package
   directions and drained
1 cup light cream
1 cup grated Parmesan cheese
   Freshly ground black pepper
   to taste

Serve It Up Penne A la Pomadora

*This is my favorite pasta.
Simple and gives me the
carbohydrates I need to practice.*

· ·

Heat the oil in a saucepan and lightly saute the onions. Add the chilies and fry 2 to 3 minutes. Add the basil to the saucepan, then increase the heat and add the tomatoes and tomato paste, breaking up the tomatoes with wooden spoon. Bring to a boil, then reduce the heat and simmer, uncovered, for about 30 minutes, until sauce is thickened. Remove from heat. Add the cooked pasta to the sauce and stir to mix. Slowly add the cream, tossing it all together in the pan. Add the Parmesan and black pepper and serve immediately. Serves 2.

(50 minutes to make - good source of protein, vitamin A, Vitamin C, and calcium.) I enjoy this pasta with a Caesar salad, a green vegetable and warm dinner rolls.

Oscar

De La Hoya

Fight Night 3 Star Combo

1	tablespoon olive oil
6	ounces New York steak, cubed
1/2	lobster tail, chopped into bite sized pieces
5	medium shrimp, peeled and cleaned
1	teaspoon minced garlic
1/4	teaspoon black pepper
1/2	cup chopped onions
1	tablespoon capers
1	tablespoon heavy cream
1	tablespoon brandy

This is my specialty before every fight... full of energy and pretty low in fat.

Boxing's "Golden Boy" is 24-0 with 20 KOs since turning pro after winning the lightweight gold medal at the 1992 Summer Olympics. He is currently the WBC welterweight champion

Heat oil in large skillet. Saute everything for about 15 minutes. Serves 1.

Smokin' Joe's Chicken

2   pound boneless chicken breast, cut into serving-size portions
1   small onion
1   clove garlic
2   tablespoons crushed red peppers
      Juice of 2 lemons
1   cup ketchup (Heinz preferably)
1   cup honey
1/4   cup diced walnuts
1   naval orange
      Fresh parsley snips

Wash chicken thoroughly and place in shallow pan. Preheat oven to 325 degrees F. Chop onion as fine as possible and crush garlic clove. Toss onion, garlic, and pepper together and sprinkle over chicken. Pour lemon juice over all. Bake at 325 degrees F. for 15 minutes. Combine honey and ketchup to make a glaze. Brush glaze over chicken, then sprinkle on walnuts. Cook an additional 15 minutes or until little juice runs out of chicken when pricked with fork. Decorate chicken with orange cut in six pieces and parsley. Serves 4.

Rock 'em, Sock 'em Rigatoni with Vodka Sauce

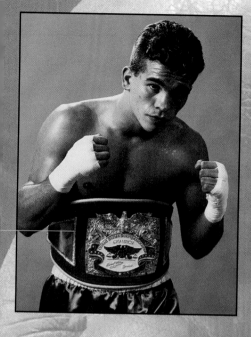

3	ounces butter
6	ounces prosciutto
4-1/2	ounces vodka
1	pint heavy cream
4	cups prepared marinara sauce
1	green or red pepper, seeded and chopped
2/3	cup grated Parmesan cheese
3	egg yolks, lightly beaten
1	pound rigatoni, cooked according to package directions and drained

Place butter and prosciutto in pan and allow to simmer. Add vodka, being careful because it could flame. Continue to simmer. Add heavy cream, marinara sauce, pepper, grated cheese and egg yolks and mix well. Place rigatoni in a large bowl and toss gently with sauce. Garnish with parsley.

Buono Appetito! Serves 4.

Real Deal Collard Greens

3-4 stalks collard greens
1   ham hock
1   teaspoon salt

• • • • • • • • • • • • • • • • • •

Chop collard greens. Place ham hock in water and let boil for one hour. Add collard greens and salt and let boil for another 45 minutes.

Macaroni and Cheese

1   16- ounce package macaroni, cooked according to package directions and drained
1   egg, beaten
1   cup milk
1/4 teaspoon black pepper
1/2 stick margarine, melted
3/4 pound cheddar cheese, shredded
Salt to taste

I have always loved this recipe whether I'm in serious training for a fight or just keeping myself in shape, my diet will always include this tasty dish of protein and carbohydrates.

• • • • • • • • • • • • • • •

While macaroni is cooking, mix remaining ingredients in a bowl. Stir in cooked macaroni. Heat oven to 400 degrees F, and bake for 45 minutes. Serve with ham hock and collard greens. Serves 4.

Holyfield

In 1992, Floyd became the only golfer to ever win events on both the Senior PGA TOUR and the PGA TOUR in the same year. He has won four major titles and more than $11 million during his career.

Raymond's Ryder Cup Spicy Chili

3	pounds shank meat, cut in 1/2 inch cubes
1/4	cup oil
2	cloves garlic, finely chopped
1	small onion, finely chopped
1-1/2	cups tomato sauce
1	10-ounce can beer
3	tablespoons chili powder
3/4	teaspoon ground cumin
1	teaspoon paprika
1	teaspoon slat
1/4	teaspoon black pepper
1/4	teaspoon cayenne pepper

Heat the oil in a large, heavy pot and add the meat, cooking over low heat until the meat turns gray. Do not let it brown. Add the garlic and onions, cover and simmer for about 8 minutes. Add the tomato sauce and beer, cover and let simmer for about 12 minutes. Mix all the remaining ingredients in a separate bowl and add them to the meat. Cover and cook for 1-1/2 to 2 hours over low heat. The meat is done when it breaks apart with a fork. The chili is better the next day, and it freezes well. Serve with rice if desired. Serves 4 to 6.

Pecan Pie

1	pie crust — homemade, unbake — small 9"
3	eggs
1/2	cup sugar
	Pinch salt
1	teaspoon vanilla
1	cup dark karo syrup
3	tablespoons melted butter (not hot)
1-2/3	cups whole (top quality) pecans

Beat eggs with fork, add rest of ingredients and mix well. Pour into shell and bake 350 for 1/2 hour. Bake on low rung of oven. Serve with sweetened whipped cream.

Hale Irwin

Irwin, a three-time U.S. Open champion, leading money winner on the 1997 Senior PGA TOUR. 20 career victories on the PGA TOUR. Has earned more than 10 million dollars in his 30 year-career.

Tee-Time Broccoli Casserole

1	10-ounce package frozen, chopped broccoli
4	tablespoons butter
1	medium onion
1	10-1/2-ounce can condensed cream of mushroom soup
1/4	cup milk
1/4	pound processed cheese, shredded or cubed
1	cup cooked rice
20	Ritz crackers (crunched)
4	tablespoons melted butter

• •

Cook broccoli according to package directions and drain. In separate pan, melt butter and brown the chopped onion. Add mushroom soup, milk and cheese. When cheese is melted, added the cooked broccoli and rice. Mix the cracker crumbs and melted butter and distribute over the top. Bake at 300 degrees F. for 20 minutes. Serves 4.

Mother's Back Nine BBQ

1   medium onion, chopped
1   green pepper, chopped
1   16-ounce can tomatoes
1   can corned beef
1   bottle catsup

Saute onion and green pepper in butter. Add remaining ingredients and simmer on low heat for one hour. Serve over English muffins. Serves 4.

These two recipes are easy for a new cook and just about foolproof - I know, I lived on them until I got married and my wife started to cook for me.

Down The Fairway Easy Rice

1   stick margarine or butter
1   cup uncooked converted rice
1   can beef consomme
1   can water
1   onion, chopped
1   dash thyme, oregano or rosemary

Mix ingredients in greased casserole and cook uncovered for 45 minutes in 350° oven. Serves 4.

Sugared Bacon Strips

This was shared with me by a dear friend and has always been the most popular item at our parties!

1/2 pound bacon, room temperature
1 cup brown sugar

Roll, pat or shake raw bacon in brown sugar and place strips on any flat pan with sides. Bake in a 275° oven for about 25 to 30 minutes, until dark brown. You may turn over once with a pincher or tongs. When bacon appears well done, remove with tongs and drain on brown paper, very thoroughly (grocery bags are very good for this). As it cools, it will get hard and can then be broken into smaller pieces or served whole. Bacon can be made earlier in the day and stored in aluminum foil, and reheated when ready to serve. Serves 4.

Arnold Palmer

Hole-In-One Spaghetti al Melone

A recipe from Venice, Italy

2	ounces butter
1	mid-size cantaloupe (peeled, seeded and cut in 1-inch cubes)
	Salt and black pepper to taste
1	tablespoon lemon juice
1	teaspoon tomato puree
1	cup heavy cream
1/2	cup shredded Parmegiano-Reggiano cheese
1	pound pasta (spaghetti, fettuccine, tonnarelli, tagliatelle or any other favorite)

Fruit is great, but golfers can not live on melon alone. When I'm not enjoying some of natures bounty, I'm in the kitchen whipping up some of my famous spaghetti. After finishing this meal, my ball always goes a bit further down the fairway.

Melt the butter in a big pan on medium heat. Add the melon cubes after butter has stopped foaming. Stir to coat the melon cubes with the butter. Saute until all the liquid has condensed. Add the salt and black pepper, lemon juice and the tomato puree. Pour in the cream and let simmer, stirring occasionally. When sauce has cooked down about halfway, it's done. Cook the pasta according to package directions and drain. Toss gently with the sauce and cheese. Serve immediately.

Serves 4. Bon Appetit!

Annika Sorenstam

Sorenstam, a two-time U.S. Women's Open winner is one of the brightest young stars in golf. The 27-year-old Swede won consecutive Vare Trophies in 1995 and 1996 for averaging the lowest score per round on the LPGA Tour.

Andretti

Zucchini Eggplant Casserole

1/3	cup olive oil
2	large onions, thinly sliced
2	eggplants, unpeeled and cubed
3	small zucchini, unpeeled and cubed
2	green peppers chopped
3	tomatoes, peeled and chopped
3	tablespoons tomato sauce
	Salt to taste
	Pepper to taste
	Accent to taste
	Garlic to taste
1	tablespoon parsley
	Pinch grated nutmeg
1/2	cup grated Parmesan cheese
4	slices Swiss or Muenster cheese

• •

Preheat oven to 350 degrees F. Saute onions and green peppers in oil. Then add eggplant, zucchini, tomatoes, and tomato sauce and seasonings and cook until vegetables are a little soft. Mix in Parmesan cheese and then spread entire mixture on the bottom of a baking pan or casserole dish. Bake at 350 degrees F. for 30 minutes. Then put 4 or more slices of cheese to cover top of casserole and bake 5 to 10 minutes longer until cheese is melted. Serves 4.

Checkered Flag Pavlova

4	egg whites
1	cup granulated sugar
1/2	teaspoon vanilla
1	teaspoon white vinegar
2	cups heavy cream
1/2	cup toasted slivered almonds
	Fresh fruit (kiwi and strawberries are perfect!)

• •

Preheat oven to 275 degrees F. Whip egg whites until they form soft peaks. Gradually add sugar, vanilla and vinegar. Continue beating until very stiff. Spread on waxed paper or brown paper on a cookie sheet in a circle, slightly smaller than desired size. Bake one hour at 275 degrees F. Turn off oven and let meringue sit for several hours to dry. Top with whipped cream, fresh fruit and toasted almonds. Serves 4.

Mario Andretti—one of the greatest drivers in the history of motorsports, Andretti has more than 100 victories in nearly every type of racing. He's won the Indy 500, Daytona 500 and a Formula One World Championship.

Michael Andretti—won five Indy Car races in 1996—the most of any driver— but fell just short of winning his second CART World Series title. Andretti, the 1991 Series winner, has 35 career victories since his rookie season in 1983.

Raceday Italian Tomatoes and Meat Sauce

1	pound 95% lean ground beef
1-1/2	cups sliced white button mushrooms
2	15-ounce cans tomato sauce, preferably low-sodium
2	28-ounce cans no-sodium tomatoes, drained and chopped
1	cup finely chopped onion
3	large garlic cloves minced
1/4	cup dry red wine
1	tablespoon chopped fresh parsley
1	teaspoon crumbled dried oregano or 2 teaspoons chopped fresh
1	teaspoon clover honey
1	teaspoon whole fennel seeds
1	teaspoon sweet paprika
1/2	teaspoon dried crumbled basil
1/2	teaspoon salt
1	large bay leaf
1	1/2 ounce packet Butter Buds
1/4	teaspoon cayenne pepper

• • • • • • • • • • • • • • • • • • • •

Spray a large non-stick saucepan with vegetable oil. Cook the ground beef over medium-high heat, breaking it up with spoon edge, until it loses its pink color, about 5 minutes. Add mushrooms and sauté briefly until they begin to give up their liquid, about 5 minutes. Reduce heat to medium-low and add remaining ingredients. Simmer 30 minutes, stirring occasionally. Use over pasta of choice. Enough sauce for 2 pounds of pasta.

The 1982 NASCAR Winston Cup Rookie of the Year, Bodine has gone on to win 18 races and more than $11 million in career earnings. His win at Watkins Glen in 1996 was Bodine's first as the owner of his own team.

Fittipaldi

Emerson, a two-time Formula One world champion (1971 & '73), also won the Indy 500 in 1988 and 1993. His nephew Christian, runner-up and rookie of the year at the 1995 Indy 500, has the tools to also become a racing legend.

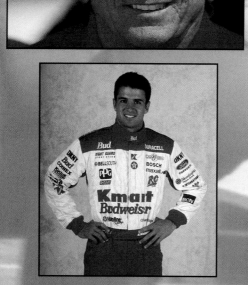

Fittipaldi Family's Grand Prix Risotto al Funghi

150	grams dried funghi
3	tablespoons olive oil
1	onion, finely chopped
2	cups Arborio rice
2	cups white wine (use already open bottle if available)
2	Knorr chicken stock cubes
1	liter water
	Dash pepper
3 to 4	tablespoon unsalted butter
3 to 4	tablespoons freshly grated Parmesan cheese

Wash the funghi under water for about 30 seconds. Place them in a bowl and add half a cup of warm water. Let stand 15 to 20 minutes or until funghi are soft and water has acquired a brown coloring.

Heat the olive oil in a large high pan. Add the chopped onion and saute until golden. Pour in the rice, stir well, and add 1 cup of white wine, covering immediately until the "sh" noise ends. Dissolve the two chicken stock cubes in the liter of water.

Add half to the rice, covering the pan again immediately. Let cook approximately 20 minutes, checking once in a while for liquid. Add more stock as necessary. When that is used up, start gradually adding the funghi water. Add funghi about 5 minutes before rice is done. Taste occasionally, and make sure the rice does not get too soggy or soft. It is very important to serve it "al dente". As soon as you feel your risotto is ready, get everybody to the table because it must be served immediately. Add a few chunks of unsalted butter, a little bit more white wine and the grated Parmesan cheese. Make sure that it is not dry. Enjoy it!!! Serves 4.

With more than 30 victories in 14 years of Indy car racing, Little Al has proudly upheld the family racing tradition. His best season came in 1994 when he won eight of 16 races, including the Indy 500, to take his second Indy Car World Series title.

Victory Lane Quesadillas

by Shelley Unser

12 flour tortillas
1   pound colby or Monterey cheese
    Salsa
    Green chili (diced or whole)

Broil flour tortilla covered in cheese with chili until bubbling. You may also cook on the top of stove in pan. Add favorite salsa. Some people prefer to add ingredients of their choice and fold the tortilla in half to make it easier to eat! This can be turned into a meal by adding any of the following: diced tomatoes, lettuce, shredded beef, chicken, guacamole, sour cream, black olives, onions, green peppers. Serves 6 to 8.

The winner of four Indianapolis 500s (1970, '71, 78 and '87), Unser led at the Brickyard for a career record 625 laps. He won three Indy Car World Series championships, the last coming in 1985, at age 46, when he narrowly outpointed his son Al, Jr.

Mom Unser's High Octane "Indy" Chili

1   pound lean pork, cut in cubes
    or ground
1   medium onion
1   clove fresh garlic
1   32-ounce can tomatoes
    1 shake oregano
    Salt to taste
1   32-ounce can mild or medium
    green chilis

Saute pork, onion and garlic together. Squeeze tomatoes through fingers and add to skillet tomato juice. Add 1 shake of oregano and salt to taste. Add green chili and simmer approximately 35 minutes. Add water if necessary. Pinto beans may be added, if desired or serve as a side dish. Serves 4 to 6.

Al **Unser, Jr.**

Al **Unser, Sr.**

Vasser

Pole Position Pork Loin Roast

4-5   pounds pork Loin roast
2-3   tablespoons crushed garlic
10   ounces Worcestershire Sauce
2   teaspoons Cholula Hot Sauce
      Lawry's Seasoning Salt to taste
      Black pepper to taste

Vasser surprised the Indy Car scene when he broke the rookie qualifying record at the 1992 Indy 500 with a speed of 222.313 MPH. His career really took off in 1996 when he won four races to take the CART World Series title.

Poke holes all over pork with a fork. Pat crushed garlic all over pork. Mix Worcestershire sauce and Cholula hot sauce together. Pour some over the bottom of a container big enough to hold pork. Season pork with Lawry's and pepper. Place pork in container and pour the remaining sauce mix over pork. Seal container and let sit in refrigerator for 24 hours. Cook on spit 25 to 30 minutes per pound on high heat. Baste with marinade every 15 to 20 minutes. Serves 8 to 10.

Jimmy Vasser

Radical Lemon Squares

Crust:

2	cups flour
6	ounces butter

Filling:

6	eggs
3	cups granulated sugar
1	cup fresh lemon juice
3/4	cup flour
3/4	cup confectioners' sugar

● ● ● ● ● ● ● ● ● ● ● ● ● ● ● ● ● ● ● ●

Cut butter into flour until mixture is the size of small peas. Pour into an 8- x 8- x 2-inch baking dish. Press down lightly until the bottom of the dish is covered. Bake at 325 degrees F. for 15 minutes.

To make filling, whisk eggs together lightly. Add the granulated sugar, lemon juice and flour and mix well. Pour over the baked crust and bake at 300 degrees F. for 40 minutes. Remove from oven and sprinkle with confectioners' sugar. Cut into squares when cold. Makes 16 2-inch squares.

X-Treme Mc Smoothie

1	cup pineapple juice
1/4	cup orange juice
1	cup strawberries, cleaned and stemmed
1	cup sliced banana
1/2	cup unflavored non-fat yogurt

● ● ● ● ● ● ● ● ● ● ● ● ● ● ● ● ● ● ●

Mix all the ingredients together in a blender and enjoy!!! Makes about 3 cups.

Perfect 10 Pasta Puttanesca

1	tablespoon olive oil
1	cup chopped onion
2	garlic cloves, minced
1-1/2	cups canned low-sodium tomatoes, drained and chopped
1	cup low-sodium tomato sauce
6	pitted large ripe olives, sliced
3	tablespoons capers
1/4	teaspoon ground red pepper
1	2-ounce can anchovies, drained (optional)
	Freshly ground black pepper to taste
6	ounces spaghetti, cooked and drained
	Grated Parmesan cheese to taste

In a large skillet, heat oil and add onion and garlic. Cook 7 to 10 minutes, until soft. Add tomatoes, tomato sauce, olives, capers, red pepper and anchovies (if you are using). Increase heat to high, and cook, stirring often, 3 to 5 minutes, until thickened. Season with black pepper. Transfer to a large serving bowl. Add spaghetti and toss gently. Top with grated Parmesan and serve. Serves 4.

Back-Flip Snickerdoodles

This is my favorite cookie of all time since I was a kid. This is a great snack if you need some immediate energy!

2 cups all-purpose flour
2 teaspoons cream of tartar
1 teaspoon baking soda
1 cup butter or margarine, salted
2 eggs
1 cups white sugar
1 cup brown sugar
1/2 cup brown sugar
1 tablespoon of cinnamon

Mix butter, white and brown sugars (excluding 1/2 cup sugar and cinnamon) until smooth. Beat in the eggs one at a time. In a separate bowl stir together the flour, cream of tartar and baking soda. Gradually add to the butter mixture. Stir well - mixing consistently. Place dough in plastic and refrigerate for 1 hour. Preheat oven to 400 degrees F. Mix together cup brown sugar and 1 tablespoon of ground cinnamon in a deep mixing bowl. Roll 1inch balls of dough into cinnamon mixture and place 2 inches apart on cookie sheets. Bake 8 to 10 minutes until lightly browned. Makes 3 dozen snickerdoodles.

Hamilton ended his four-year reign as men's figure skating world champion with a gold medal at the 1984 Winter Olympics. He went on to skate professionally and has been a CBS broadcaster since 1987.

Triple Axle Microwave Vegetable Sauce

1   cup thin diagonal carrot slices
1   cup matchstick-size strips red
     bell pepper
1   cup thinly sliced zucchini
1   cup thinly sliced yellow crookneck
     squash
1   teaspoon Oriental sesame oil
2   tablespoons minced peeled
     fresh ginger
1   tablespoon reduced-sodium
     soy sauce
     Salt and pepper to taste
1/4 cup chopped fresh chives

• • • • • • • • • • • • • • • • • • • •

Arrange vegetables on a large microwave-safe plate. Cover plate tightly with plastic wrap. Microwave on high until vegetables begin to soften, about 1-1/2 minutes. Heat oil in a large non-stick skillet over medium-high heat. Add ginger, and saute 30 seconds. Sprinkle with soy sauce, season with salt and pepper. Mix in chives. Pour over the vegetables and serve. Serves 3 to 4.

Kristi Yamaguchi

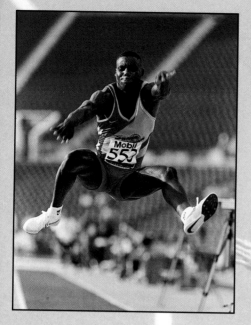

Olympic Black-Eyed Peas and Brown Rice

After a day of running, sprinting and long-jumping, I need something that's easy to prepare and good for my body. This recipe has been with me from Los Angeles to Seoul and Barcelona to Atlanta.

Peas:

1	pound black-eyed peas, washed well
1/2	cup chopped onions
1	cup chopped tomatoes
1	cup seeded, chopped red bell pepper
2	cups diced potato
1	tablespoon Tony's "Crackers" Creole Seasoning (if unavailable combine 1-1/2 teaspoons each cayenne pepper and salt)
1	teaspoon dry basil leaves (or 2 teaspoons fresh)
6	cups water

Combine all ingredients in a 4-quart pot. Bring to a boil and simmer uncovered 45 minutes to 1 hour, until tender. Stir occasionally. Serves 6

Rice:

1-1/2	cups brown rice
1/4	cup chopped onion
1/4	cup chopped tomatoes
1/4	cup seeded, chopped bell pepper
3	cups water
	Salt to taste

• •

Combine all ingredients in a 3-quart pot. Bring to a boil, cover and simmer about 30 minutes, or until rice is tender. Serves 6.

Long Jump Lemon Chicken

My favorite food after any big race!

1	12 ounce chicken breast
	Salt and pepper to taste
1	tablespoon flour
2	tablespoons olive oil
1	tablespoon capers
3	tablespoons artichoke hearts
	Juice of 1 lemon
4	tablespoons chicken stock
1	tablespoon butter
1	roasted potato, cut into 5 wedges

I've picked-up a few cooking tips along my many travels and this is absolutely my favorite. It's got flavor and some KICK! When you feel like getting creative in the kitchen and looking for something a little different, pull out this easy recipe and enjoy.

Lightly season chicken with salt and pepper. Dust with flour and saute in hot oil until golden brown. Discard oil. Add capers and artichoke hearts and cook over medium low heat until chicken is tender. Remove chicken and artichoke hearts from pan and keep warm. Add lemon juice to pan and deglaze by bringing to a boil and scraping sides of pan gently. Add chicken stock and butter. Reduce till sauce is thickened. Pour over chicken and serve with roasted potato. Serve 1.

Record Breaking Baked Fish with Vegetables

1	pound flounder fillets (or another firm-fleshed fish, such as cod)
1	tablespoon vegetable oil
1	cup onions, sliced
2	cups zucchini, sliced
1	cup green peppers, seeded and sliced
3/4	cup chopped tomatoes
3	tablespoons dry sherry (optional)
1	tablespoon lemon juice
1/4	teaspoon salt
1/2	teaspoon ground basil
1/4	teaspoon black pepper, freshly ground
	Dash hot pepper sauce
1/4	cup grated Parmesan cheese

My diet is essential for maintaining top competitive form and this recipe gets me rolling out of the blocks. Whether you spice it up, or dress it down, you can't go wrong.

• •

Cut fillets into serving-sized pieces and place in a single layer in a greased 9-inch baking dish. Heat the oil in a skillet and saute onion, zucchini and green pepper until tender, then spoon over fillets. Top with tomatoes. Combine sherry, lemon juice, salt, basil, pepper and pepper sauce. Pour over fillets. Bake, uncovered, in preheated 350-degree F. oven for 25 to 30 minutes. Remove vegetables and fish to heated platter. Sprinkle with Parmesan cheese. Serve over rice. Pour pan juices over fish and vegetables if desired. Serves 4.

All-Around Brownies

The first time I met my wife Kris, she made these unbelievable brownies for me and they have been my favorite ever since. My personal favorite is to serve them with a big scoop of vanilla ice cream on top.

4	1-ounce squares unsweetened chocolate, coarsely chopped
2	tablespoons (1/4 stick) unsalted butter
4	eggs
2	teaspoons vanilla extract
2	cups sugar
1	cup all-purpose flour
1/2	teaspoon salt
1	cup chopped walnuts
1	12 ounce package mini semisweet chocolate chips
	Confectioners' sugar (optional)

• •

Preheat the oven to 325 degrees F. grease a 9-by-13 inch baking pan. Combine the unsweetened chocolate and the butter in the top of a double boiler. Stir over hot but not boiling water until melted and smooth. Remove from heat and set aside.

In the bowl of a food processor, process the eggs, vanilla, sugar, flour, baking powder, and salt until smooth. Add the melted chocolate and process until smooth. Add the walnuts and chocolate chips and pulse briefly to mix. Pour the batter into the prepared pan and bake until a toothpick inserted in the center comes out clean, 25 to 30 minutes. Invert onto a rack and cool completely. Sprinkle with confectioners' sugar if desired. Cut into squares and serve with vanilla ice cream.

Makes about 30, 2 inch brownies. For chewier brownies, bake 20 minutes.

Slim Speed Skating Saltimbocca

4	boneless chicken breasts, pounded to 1/4 inch thick
1	ounce skim mozzarella cheese
2	ounces very fully cooked ham
3	pounds fine bread crumbs
1	tablespoon parmesan cheese (grated)
1	teaspoon parsley flakes
1/2	teaspoon oregano
1/2	teaspoon pepper & garlic powder
1/2	cup skim milk

● ●

Divide ham and mozzarella equally and roll up inside of each chicken breast, using wooden tooth picks to hold the rolls together. Mix all the dry ingredients together in a medium bowl; put milk into another bowl. Dip each chicken roll in milk, then roll in crumb mixture. Place in a baking pan and bake uncovered at 350 degrees for approximately 25 minutes, or until chicken is thoroughly cooked. Serve with rice and steamed broccoli or asparagus. Serves 4.

Cutting-Edge Peanut Butter Chocolate Squares

1	1-pound box confectioner's sugar
1-1/2	cups smooth or crunchy Skippy peanut butter
1-1/2	cups graham cracker crumbs
1-1/2	sticks melted margarine
8 to 12	ounces semi-sweet chocolate bits
1/2	stick margarine (additional)

Mix the sugar, peanut butter, graham cracker crumbs and melted margarine together well and press into bottom of a 13 x 9-inch pan. Press mixture down firmly. Melt chocolate chips and the 1/2 stick margarine together in a saucepan and pour over the firmly-packed crust. Set aside until completely cool then cut into squares. Yield will vary according to size of squares.

Peanut Butter Cookies

2	sticks butter
1	cup Skippy peanut butter
1/2	salt
1	cup sugar
1	cup brown sugar (firmly packed)
2	eggs, well-beaten
1	tablespoon milk
2	cups sifted flour
1/2	teaspoon baking soda

Combine butter, salt and peanut butter and mix well; gradually add sugar and brown sugar and cream firmly after each addition. Add eggs, milk and mix well. Sift flour and soda together and add with mixture. Drop by teaspoon on greased cookie sheet. Flatten with fork. Bake at 325 degrees F. for 15 to 20 minutes. Makes about 4 dozen cookies.

Senior members of the gold-medal winning 1996 U.S. women's gymnastics team, Miller won an individual gold on the balance beam, and Strug cemented the team gold with a courageous vault on an injured ankle.

Triple Tumbling Chicken Teriyaki

The following meal is one of my favorites:

3	tablespoons sesame seeds (we toast them in a dry skillet before using)
2	tablespoons reduced-sodium soy sauce
2	tablespoons honey
1	teaspoon Oriental sesame oil (optional)
1	teaspoon minced fresh ginger
1	clove garlic, minced
?	teaspoon black pepper
3	skinless, boneless chicken breast halves (4 ounces each), cut into 1 inch chunks

In a medium bowl, combine sesame seeds, soy sauce, honey, sesame oil, ginger, garlic and pepper. Mix well. Set aside 2 tablespoons of marinade. Add the chicken to the remaining marinade in the bowl and stir to coat. Cover bowl with plastic wrap; refrigerate for 30 minutes, stirring occasionally. Preheat broiler. Remove chicken from marinade and place in a broiler pan. Discard the marinade in bowl. Broil 5 inches from heat, basting with the reserved marinade and turning once, until done, about 10 to 12 minutes. Garnish chicken with chopped scallions, if desired. Serve immediately. Serves 2

Blueberry Olympic Bran Muffins

Shannon Miller

The secret of these muffins is the buttermilk, which makes them rise light and fluffy. Make an extra batch and freeze for a brunch treat the following weekend.

2	cups wheat or oat bran
2	cups whole wheat flour
1	cup blueberries, fresh or thaw frozen ones
1-1/2	teaspoons baking soda
1/3	cup molasses
1/3	cup honey
2	cups buttermilk
	Margarine, for coating tins

In a large bowl, combine bran, flour, blueberries and baking soda. Stir together molasses, honey and buttermilk, then add bran mixture and mix until well combined. Let stand for 20 minutes. Lightly oil a 12 cup muffin tin. Preheat oven to 350 degrees F. Fill muffin cups two thirds full of batter and bake until muffins spring back slightly when pressed in the center, about 30 minutes. Remove from pan and serve warm. Makes 12 muffins.

Kerri Strug

Conner, a gold-medalist on the parallel bars at the 1984 Olympics, scored his biggest win when he married Comaneci, who won a total of five golds, four silvers and a bronze as a gymnast for Romania at the 1976 and 1980 Olympics.

Tumbling Eggplant Spread

(Romanian "Salata de Vinete")

This is an eggplant spread ideal on crackers, rye-krisps, or cocktail bread squares. It is a traditional Romanian recipe, and Bart's favorite. The true traditional Romanian style "Salata de Vinete" is served with roasted red peppers on the side. Enjoy!

2	medium eggplants, unpeeled and ripe
2/3	cup vegetable oil
1	medium white onion, finely chopped
4	tablespoons "light" mayonnaise
1	teaspoon Dijon mustard
	Pinch salt

Preheat oven to 400 degrees F.. Poke holes with a fork all over eggplants. Place the eggplants on a non-stick cooking sheet in the oven and bake for about 80 minutes, turning the eggplants every 20 minutes or so, to be sure they are baked on all sides. Eggplants should be mushy when they are finished baking.

Carefully put the eggplants in a zip-locked bag for ten minutes. Remove them from the bag, peal off the skin and discard. Put the eggplant "meat" into a strainer and drain it for about ten minutes. On a cutting board, chop the eggplant until it becomes mashed like potatoes, and put it in a bowl.

Stir with a wooden spoon, while slowly adding the oil. At this point the mixture will look pretty firm. Add the light mayonnaise and mustard. Stir until the mixture is complete. Add onion to the mixture, season with salt to taste. Refrigerate mixture for about two hours. Makes 4 to 6 cups.

Milligan's Mysterious Downhill Morels

The reason this recipe is so mysterious is that the morels are very difficult to find and we're never sure if we're going to find them when we go hunting for them. There is only a short period of time during the spring when they are available. The other thing is that some years are better than others for harvesting mushrooms, and our location always remains a secret, the way a favorite fishing hole remains a secret. We have our spot for finding mushrooms and all I can say is, "It's in Idaho."

1/2	pound morel mushrooms
2	eggs, beaten
10	soda crackers
2	tablespoons butter

• •

Clean and cut each mushroom in half lengthwise. Drain on paper towels. Beat the eggs slightly. Crush the soda crackers as finely as possible. (We always put the crackers in a plastic bag and crush them with a rolling pin.) If preferred, you may substitute a 1/2 cup of flour for the soda crackers. Dip the mushrooms in the eggs, then roll them in the cracker crumbs. Heat butter in a skillet and saute on both sides till golden brown. Serve immediately as the entree or vegetable dish or just a snack. Serves 3 to 4.

Super G. Tortilgioni with Tomato and Parmesan

1   **pound (400 grams) Barilla tortilgioni**
      Fresh basil to taste
      Fresh mint to taste
4   **tablespoons olive oil**
1   **pound (400 grams) fresh tomatoes, peeled and chopped**
3-1/2 **ounces (100 grams) aged Parmesan cheese, grated**
      Salt and pepper to taste

Bring a large pot of salted water to a boil and cook the pasta al dente. In the meantime, chop a handful of fresh basil leaves and a few fresh mint leaves. Heat 2 tablespoons of the oil in a large pan and saute the chopped tomatoes for about a minute. Add a pinch of salt, the chopped herbs, and the drained, cooked pasta to the tomatoes. Quickly stir the contents of the pan, allowing the flavors to meld. Sprinkle with the grated Parmesan cheese, add pepper to taste, and drizzle with the remaining 2 tablespoons olive oil before serving. Serves 4.

There is nothing that I love more than these recipes! I eat pasta everyday, sometimes twice a day, double portions, since it's not only my most favorite meal, but also one of my most important sources of energy when I'm training.

Olympic Village Penne Primavera

• • • • • • • • • • • • • • • • • • • •

4   **tablespoons olive oil**
2   **garlic cloves, minced**
1   **carrot, peeled and diced**
2   **zucchini, diced**
1   **onion, diced**
1   **yellow pepper, seeded and diced**
1   **green pepper, seeded and diced**
1   **small eggplant, diced**
1   **celery stalk, diced**
1   **pound Barilla penne**
1   **bunch fresh basil, chopped**
2   **tablespoons grated Parmegiano cheese**
      Pepper to taste

Heat olive oil in a large skillet. Add the garlic and vegetables and saute until all is tender. Cook the pasta al dente in abundant salted water, drain, and add to the pan with the vegetables. Stir briefly until the flavors meld. Sprinkle with fresh, chopped basil leaves and grated Parmegiano cheese. Add pepper to taste, and drizzle with remaining 2 tablespoons olive oil. Serves 4.

Tomba "LA Bomba" burst onto the alpine ski scene at the 1988 Winter Olympics when he won gold in the slalom and the giant slalom. Tomba recently repeated that feat at the 1996 World Alpine Ski Championships.

Dan O'Brien

Decath-Licious Chicken Fajitas

2 cups leftover roast chicken (or 1 pound boneless chicken cutlets)
1 tablespoon Cajun seasoning
 Juice from 1 lemon
1 tablespoon bottled Italian dressing (fat-free is fine)
1/2 medium green pepper, cut in julienne strips
1/2 small red onion, cut in thin rings
4 tortillas (warmed in oven)
1/2 cup bottled salsa
 Sour cream (optional)
 Chopped cilantro leaves

The world's best decathlete since 1991, O'Brien finally won his Olympic gold in 1996. Although he failed to qualify for the U.S. team in 1992, he did set the world record just one month after the 1992 Summer Olympics.

Cut chicken into thin strips, mix with seasoning and lemon juice and let stand 10 minutes. (If using uncooked chicken, rub with seasoning and grill 5 minutes per side until done. Cut into strips, add lemon juice and let stand 10 minutes.

Heat the dressing in a non-stick pan. Add pepper and onion and heat until softened. Add chicken strips and cook, stirring, until heated through. Pile one-fourth of filling on each tortilla. Add salsa, sour cream and cilantro and fold up. Serves 4.

Fast Pitch California Garlic Burgers

1-1/2 pounds lean ground beef
1-1/2 cups soft bread crumbs
1/4   cup chopped onion
2   eggs, slightly beaten
2   teaspoons sugar
2   tablespoons chopped green pepper
3   teaspoons soy sauce
1   glove garlic, crushed
3   teaspoons beer (your choice)
     Dash salt
     Hamburger buns

• •

Combine ground beef with the remaining ingredients, except buns, and mix well. Shape into patties (6 to 8 depending on size). BBQ on the grill to desired doneness. Place burger on toasted sesame seed bun. Top with your favorite condiments. Serves 4 to 6.

Julie Smith #15

Spiked Penne A la Vodka

Unbeatable, simple, delicious. This dish has a version with slight variations all over Italy. The vodka adds a slight favor to the sauce after the alcohol cooks off. This recipe was given to me by Sam Armato, my boyfriend's father, and it is delicious!

2   shallots, sliced
1/4   cup olive oil
1   teaspoon red pepper flakes
2   ounces vodka
1/2   cup heavy cream
1   16-ounce can whole plum tomatoes,
        undrained, processed in blender or
        food processor for 5 seconds
2   tablespoons parsley, chopped
1   pound penne, cooked according to
        package directions and drained

• •

Saute shallots in olive oil until tender. Add red pepper flakes. Turn up heat, and then add vodka, which should flambe. Continue for 30 seconds, then add cream and tomatoes. Simmer for about 10 minutes, stirring occasionally. Toss gently with cooked penne in serving bowl. Garnish with parsley and serve. Serves 4.

Splish-Splash Apricot Chicken

1-1/2	pounds boneless breast of chicken
1	cup bottled Russian or catalina salad dressing
2	teaspoons mayonnaise
1	packet Lipton onion soup mix
3/4	cup bottled apricot preserves

Preheat oven to 350 degrees F. Place chicken in a shallow baking pan. Stir the dressing, mayonnaise, soup mix and preserves together and pour on top of chicken. Bake for one hour at 350 degrees F. Serve over brown or white rice. Serves 3 to 4.

Penny
VanDyken USA

Corner Kick Chocolate Chess Pie

I personally think it is best with ice cream and absolutely must be served warm. If not all eaten at once, as I usually do, it is possible to refrigerate and then warm later in a microwave. Don't cook too long in the micro though (no longer than 30 secs) or you'll end up with a black mush. I'm not sure this dish falls into any athlete's diet table, but it is a simple and outstanding treat nonetheless! Enjoy!

1	stick butter
2	squares semi-sweet chocolate
2	eggs slightly beaten
1	cup sugar
1	teaspoon vanilla
	Dash of salt
1	8- or 9-inch unbaked pie crust

Preheat oven to 350 degrees F. Melt the butter and chocolate together. Mix the eggs, sugar, vanilla and salt together. Blend into the butter-chocolate mixture, then pour into the pie shell. Bake 35 minutes at 350 degrees F. Serve warm topped with whipped cream or ice cream. Makes 1 8- or 9-inch pie.

Jason C Kreis

Chesapeake Bay Crab Cakes with Sauce Remoulade

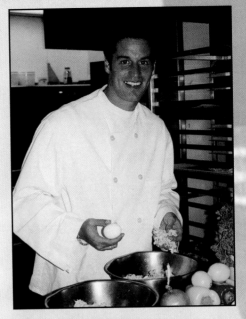

Crab Cakes:

1-2/3	pounds jumbo lump crabmeat
2	tablespoons soybean oil
1/2	green bell pepper, seeded and chopped
1/2	red bell pepper, seeded and chopped
1/2	small white onion, chopped
2	egg yolks
1	teaspoon Dijon mustard
2	drops Tabasco sauce
4	drops Worcestershire sauce
1/2	teaspoon lemon juice
1	ounce bread crumbs
3	tablespoons butter (approximately)
	Parsley sprigs for garnish
	Lemon wedges for garnish

When I returned to the United States to play in Major League Soccer last year, after six years in England, I was dying for a good steak, which is almost impossible to find in London. As a result I visited the best steakhouse in Washington D.C., and fell in love with the crabcakes of all things, a regional specialty. There is nothing more delicious than a sweet Chesapeake Bay crabcake after a long, hard workout. Indeed, picking the crabmeat from the shell is a workout unto itself.

Pick over crabmeat thoroughly and discard any shell. Heat 1 tablespoon oil in a pan and sauté peppers and onion until cooked throughout. Cool and drain. Place egg yolks in bowl. Add Dijon mustard, Tabasco sauce, Worcestershire sauce and lemon juice. Mix well. Stir in remaining tablespoon soybean oil slowly. Add the crabmeat, pepper mixture and bread crumbs. Mix thoroughly, then shape into 8 evenly-sized cakes. Melt butter in pan and sauté over medium-high heat until golden and cooked throughout, about 5 minutes per side. Serve garnished with lemon wedges and parsley sprigs and remoulade sauce (below). Serves 6 to 8.

Remoulade Sauce:

1/4	stalk celery	2	drops Worcestershire sauce
1	small scallion	1	pinch prepared horseradish
1/2	bay leaf	1	pinch fresh thyme
1/2	hard-cooked egg	2	pinches parsley
1/4	teaspoon lemon juice	1/2	teaspoon paprika
1	tablespoon Creole mustard	1/4	teaspoon cayenne
1	tablespoon ketchup	1	pinch salt
1	teaspoon champagne or white wine	1	pinch pepper
1	drop Tabasco sauce	2	tablespoons vegetable oil

Process celery, scallion and bay leaf together in food processor. Add the remaining ingredients except oil and mix well. Slowly add in oil and process until well emulsified. Makes about 1/3 cup.

John Harkes

With midfielders Foudy and Akers controlling the pace, the U.S. Women's National Soccer Team have dominated international soccer in the 90s. They helped the U.S. team win the inaugural women's soccer gold medal at the 1996 Olympics.

Mom's Gold Medal Marinara

1	pound turkey sausage, sliced (or other sausage if preferred)
1/2	cup chopped onions
2	cloves garlic, minced
8	ounces mushrooms, sliced
1/2	cup cooked broccoli, chopped
1	green pepper, seeded and sliced
1	8-ounce can tomato sauce
1	28-ounce can crushed tomatoes
	Fresh basil to taste
	Black pepper to taste

Very easy and very good. It's even better the next day with seasoning.

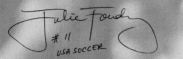

Cook turkey sausage in a skillet until browned on all sides. Drain excess grease. Add chopped onions and garlic and saute until onions are golden, about 5 minutes. Add mushrooms, green pepper and broccoli (or substitute your favorite vegetables for the pepper and broccoli). Cook vegetables 5 minutes, then add the tomato sauce and crushed tomatoes. Add fresh basil and black pepper. Bring to a boil and then turn to low and let simmer 15 minutes. Serve with rice or pasta. Enough for 1 pound of pasta, and doubles easily.

Sue-Sue The Rocket's Apple Crisp

10	medium apples	2/3	cup granulated sugar
3/4	cup flour	1/3	cup brown sugar
1	teaspoon cinnamon	1/2	cup butter, melted

Preheat oven to 350 degrees F. Peel and core apples. Slice in quarters then cut quarters into thin slices. Spread evenly in a 5 x 7-inch non-stick baking pan. Mix flour, cinnamon and sugars in a bowl. Add melted butter and stir until thoroughly mixed. Sprinkle evenly on top of sliced apples and bake at 350 degrees F. for 45 minutes. Top with vanilla ice cream or non-fat Cool Whip, then chow down. Serves 6.

Historically, my first choice for desserts was to reach for something chocolatey and rich, but since I became sick with Chronic Fatigue Immune Dysfunction Syndrome (CFIDS), I have been forced to change my diet dramatically. Suffice it to say, chocolate is not on the list. So Sue, my stepmom made me apple crisp as my birthday cake last year and it has remained my favorite ever since.

Bouncin' Jugglin' Jello

1   3-ounce package cherry-flavored gelatin mix
2   cups water

Place gelatin mix in bowl and slowly add 1 cup boiling water. Stir 3 minutes or until mix is completely dissolved. Add 1 cup of cold water and stir. Cover and refrigerate for four hours or until firm to the touch. Serve cold with fresh whipped cream. Serves 4.

Alexi Lalas

World-recognized for his heady play and head of hair, Lalas is the U.S. National Soccer Team's best defender and best-known player. He has played in more than 90 matches for the national team and is a member of the New England Revolution of the MLS.

World Cup Chicken

The all-time leading goal-scorer on the U.S. National Soccer Team, Wynalda has also been a star on foreign soil; he was the first U.S. player to succeed in Germany's toughest league, the Bundesliga.

4-5   boneless, skinless chicken breast, cut in bite-size pieces
2   tablespoons oil
3   cloves garlic, minced

Sauce:
2/3   cup dry sherry or chicken broth
2/3   cup soy sauce
2/3   cup brown sugar
1/4   teaspoon crushed red pepper, optional
2   teaspoons corn starch
2   tablespoons water

Heat oil in skillet and saute chicken on medium high until lightly browned on all sides. Remove chicken and add a little more oil, if necessary. Saute garlic for one minute, stirring carefully so it doesn't burn. Add sherry or broth, soy sauce, brown sugar and red pepper. Place chicken back into mixture in skillet, cover lightly. Simmer over low heat for about 20-25 minutes. Don't let sauce cook down. If necessary add 1-2 tablespoons of water. After about 20 minutes mix corn starch and water together and add to chicken. Stir constantly as the mixture thickens. Serve chicken and sauce over rice or noodles with a vegetable and rolls and butter. Serves 4.

Smooth Talking Dolmathes

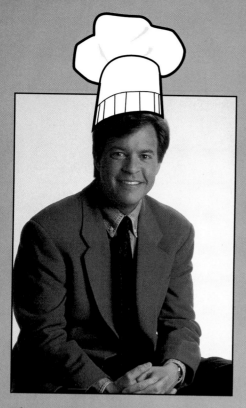

1 pound ground sirloin
2 eggs, beaten (can substitute Eggbeaters)
1 medium onion, chopped
1/2 cup uncooked rice
1/4 cup chopped parsley
1 tablespoon fresh mint leaves
1/4 cup ice water
  Salt and pepper to taste
  Mix above ingredients together in large bowl, and set aside
1 32-ounce can chicken broth
  Fresh grape leaves or 1 jar or can in brine

Sauce:
3 eggs (can substitute Eggbeaters)
3 lemons
  Hot broth from Dolmathes

If using fresh grapes leaves, soak them in hot water for 5 minutes to soften. If using jar or can, rinse in warm water.

Remove hard stem ends, and place leaves shiny side down. Put small amount of meat mixture in center of each leaf, roll, then fold in side to seal ends. Place plate over top to hold firmly in place. Layer stuffed leaves in a saucepan. Pour chicken broth over leaves, cover and cook 3/4 to 1 hour.

While grape leaves are cooking, beat 3 eggs. Add the juice of 3 lemons. Slowly add hot broth, beating constantly. Sauce should be fluffy and foamy. Add to Dolmathes. Serves 6 to 8.

My Personal Favorite Recipe

I have never cooked a meal in my life (the honest truth). Hence, this is my favorite recipe.

1.) Identify your town's best pizzeria.
2.) Call to order delivery of savory thick crust pie with extra cheese.
3.) Wait 20-30 minutes.
4.) Answer doorbell.
5.) Pay tab/with generous tip.
6.) Pour beverage.
7.) Consume & enjoy!

Bob Costas

All-Pro Hawaiian Chicken

4 cups soy sauce
1 cup granulated sugar
1 cup brown sugar
2 cups mild rice vinegar
2 cups sliced ginger root
1 12-ounce can crushed pineapple
5 pounds chicken pieces,
   skin removed

• •

Prepare marinade in a mixing bowl large enough to hold all chicken pieces. Mix soy sauce and sugars with a whisk. Stir in rice vinegar, sliced ginger and pineapple. Add your favorite skinless chicken. Thighs, breasts and drumsticks are usually preferred. Marinate up to 5 hours. Taste will be stronger as marinating time increases. Refrigerate if marinating for more than 1 hour and do not exceed 5 hours. Baste often when cooking. Can be cooked in oven in 1 layer in shallow roasting pan, but tastes best grilled. Baste frequently with marinade. Serves 6 to 8.

Note: Amount of sugars may be increased if a sweeter marinade is desired.

Gifford

Before joining ABC as a broadcaster in 1971, Gifford was a star halfback and flanker for the New York Giants, playing in seven Pro Bowls from 1952-64. He was named NFL Player of the Year in 1956 when he caught 51 passes and rushed for 819 yards.

Dick Enberg

Play-by-Play En-Burgers

1/2	pound bacon
1	16-ounce can B&M baked beans
2	medium onions, diced
1	cup brown sugar
1	teaspoon mustard
	Salt and pepper to taste
1-1/2	pounds ground beef
4	slices cheddar cheese
4	hamburger buns

Inducted in 1996 to the National Sportswriters and Sportscasters Hall of Fame, Enberg had long before left his mark on sports television with his expert coverage of Olympic events and the NFL for NBC.

Fry bacon and remove from grease. Add the beans, half the onion, the brown sugar and mustard to the bacon grease. Add salt and pepper to taste. Simmer until onions are tender. Dice cooked bacon into small pieces and add to bean mixture.

Divide the meat into patties, and cook hamburgers to taste. Melt cheddar cheese on top. Toast hamburger buns.

Serve bean mixture on top of hamburger, topped with remaining onions. Use buns on side as "scoopers". Enjoy! Serves 4.

Baby Back, Back, Back Pork Ribs

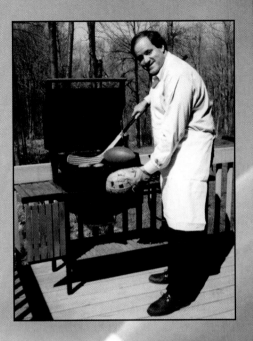

6   pounds baby pork back ribs
2   cups water

Sauce:
4   cups tomato ketchup
    (32-ounce bottle)
1/3 cup finely chopped onion
1/4 cup brown sugar
3   tablespoons lemon juice
3   tablespoons rum
3   tablespoons Worcestershire sauce
2   tablespoons liquid smoke
2   teaspoons Tabasco sauce

I visit Idaho to white-water raft the Salmon River with my brother and his family. My brother's wife, Kate, is a fantastic cook and she makes this, my favorite dish, when I'm in town.

. . . .

Preheat oven to 350. Cut rib slabs in half, leaving 6 to 8 ribs per piece. Arrange ribs evenly in a large roasting pan, and add 2 cups of water. Cover pan tightly with foil or lid to prevent steam from escaping. Bake for 3 hours, then drain and discard liquid. Two hours into the baking time, combine all the sauce ingredients in a large saucepan. Simmer over low heat for 1 hour. Prepare barbeque coals. Cover ribs with sauce, reserving about 1 1/2 cups for serving. Cook on barbecue approximately 5 minutes per side, or until charred. Serve at once, with reserved sauce on the side. Serves 6 to 8.

Chris Berman

Chris Berman

Berman has been with ESPN since one month after its inception in 1979. He is best known for his NFL and baseball coverage.

Mike

Fratello

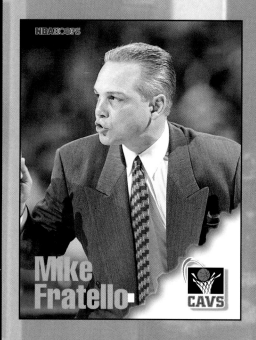

Pasta Czar Fratello

1/3	cup extra virgin olive oil
1/2	cup chopped shallots
3	garlic cloves, chopped
	Salt and pepper to taste
1	cup chicken broth
2	cups escarole or Swiss chard, finely chopped
2	tablespoon butter
1	pound linguine
3	ounces Absolut vodka
2	tablespoons chopped fresh parsley

Heat oil in skillet. Saute shallots and garlic for 5 minutes. Add salt and pepper to taste, broth and escarole. Cook over low heat for 10 minutes. Add the butter and cook, stirring, 1 minute. Cook linguine to the al dente stage, drain and add to pan. Pour in vodka. Stir for 2 minutes on high heat. Serve topped with parsley. Serves 4.

Mike Fratello

Broadcast Booth Mixed Vegetables

Vegetables:

1   10-ounce package frozen green peas
1   10-ounce package frozen lima beans
1   10-ounce package frozen
     French style green beans

• •

Cook each vegetable according to package directions, drain well, and combine in a large bowl.

Sauce:

1   cup mayonnaise
2-1/2   teaspoons Worcestershire sauce
2   teaspoons olive oil
1   small grated yellow onion
2   hard-cooked eggs, mashed
1/4   teaspoon dry or prepared mustard

• •

Combine sauce ingredients and refrigerate. While vegetables are hot, pour cold sauce over them and serve. Serves 6. Note: Sauce can be used on cold vegetables as well. Makes about 1-1/4 cups sauce.

Thanks to a keen baseball mind, McCarver spent 23 years as a major league catcher. Now, as a sportscasting veteran, he puts his hardball intellect to work for the Fox Saturday Baseball Game of the Week.

James Brown

Legendary Football Cake

3/4	cup Dutch-process cocoa
1/2	cup boiling water
3	sticks unsalted butter, plus more for pans
1/4	cup sugar
1	tablespoon vanilla extract
4	large eggs, lightly beaten
3	cups sifted cake flour
1	teaspoon baking soda
1/2	teaspoon salt
1	cup milk

Preheat oven to 350 degrees F. Butter three 8 x 2-inch cake pans and cover bottoms with parchment. If desired, dust bottoms and sides with some additional cocoa and tap out excess. Sift cocoa, add boiling water and mix well. Let cool. Cream butter on low in electric mixer. Gradually beat in the sugar until light and fluffy, about 3 to 4 minutes, scraping down sides twice. Beat in vanilla. Add eggs gradually, beating between each addition until batter is no longer slick. Sift flour, baking soda, and salt. Whisk together the cocoa mixture with the milk. With mixer on low speed, add flour mixture alternately with cocoa mixture, a little of each at a time, starting and ending with the flour. Divide evenly into the three pans. Bake 35 to 45 minutes, rotating the pans during baking, if needed, until a cake tester or toothpick inserted in centers comes out clean. Cool on racks. When ready to assemble, remove papers from bottoms of cakes. Save the prettiest layer for the top. Place one layer on a serving platter, spread with 1-1/2 cups of the chocolate frosting. Repeat with second layer, then top with third. Cover sides and top of cake with remaining 3 cups frosting. Makes 3 8-inch layers.

• •

Chocolate Frosting:

24	ounces (2 bags) semisweet chocolate morsels
4	cups heavy cream
1	teaspoon light corn syrup

Place chocolate and cream in heavy saucepan. Cook over low heat, stirring constantly, until combined and thickened, 20 to 23 minutes. Increase heat to medium low, and cook, stirring, 3 minutes more. Remove from heat, stir in corn syrup. Transfer to a large metal bowl and refrigerate. Check every 15 to 20 minutes, stirring each time, until cool enough to spread, about 2 hours. Spread the icing as soon as it is sufficiently chilled. It will keep its shape well on cake. Spread on cooled moist devil's food cake. Makes 6 cups.

Howie Long's Humbling Apple Pie

2	cups flour
1/2	tablespoon sugar
1	tablespoon salt
5/6	cup shortening
1/4	cup water
1	tablespoon cider vinegar
1	egg

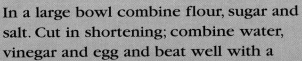

In a large bowl combine flour, sugar and salt. Cut in shortening; combine water, vinegar and egg and beat well with a fork; add egg mixture to flour mixture. Mix until pastry holds together. Divide dough into 2 balls. Cover and chill for at least 2 hours. Roll each crust out until crust is 2 inches larger than pie plate.

Dough can be made ahead of time. Wrap dough tightly and refrigerate up to 2 weeks, or freeze up to 2 months. Thaw frozen dough in refrigerator for 2 hours. Makes two crusts.

Apple Pie Filling

3/4	cup of brown sugar
3/4	cup sugar
1	tablespoon cornstarch
1	teaspoon cinnamon
1	tablespoon lemon juice
1	tablespoon butter
6	cups sliced pippin or granny Smith apples

Mix the sugars and cornstarch. Toss with apples, cinnamon and lemon juice. Place in pastry lined pie plate. Dot with butter and cover with top crust. Seal and flute edge, cut slits in the top of dough. Preheat oven to 425 degrees F. Bake 1/2 hour with foil around edges remove foil last 15 minutes. Bake pie 45 to 50 minutes, until pie is bubbling in the center.

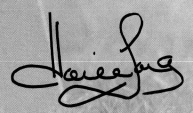

Howie Long joined Fox after a 13-year career as a defensive end with the Raiders that included eight Pro Bowl selections.

Millen, the only player to ever win Super Bowl rings with three different teams (Raiders, Redskins, 49ers), was best known for his intensity and bone-crushing tackles. He now pairs with Pat O'Brien on CBS radio as the best football tandem on the air.

Gridiron Seafood Lasagne

1	large onion, chopped	1/2	cup dry white wine
2	tablespoons butter	1	pound cooked deveined medium shrimp
8	ounces cream cheese		
2	cups ricotta cheese	1	pound crabmeat, picked over
1	large egg, beaten		
2	teaspoons basil	1	pound scallops
	Pepper to taste	1/4	grated Parmesan cheese (to taste)
2	10-ounce cans condensed cream of mushroom soup (set 1/2 cup aside)	8	large lasagne noodles
		12	ounces shredded mozzarella cheese
1/3	cup milk		

The day before serving, saute onion in butter. Pour into bowl with cream cheese, ricotta cheese, egg, basil, and pepper. Mix together well. In a separate bowl, mix together cream of mushroom soup, milk, white wine, shrimp, crabmeat, scallops and Parmesan cheese. Cook lasagne noodles as directed on package, drain and set aside. Pour the reserved 1/2 cup of cream of mushroom soup into the bottom of a large lasagne pan. Then place 4 cooked lasagne noodles over the soup. Next take half the cream cheese mixture and spread over the noodles. Top with half the mushroom soup/seafood mixture, followed by half the shredded mozzarella. Begin a second layer, starting with the lasagne noodles and continuing as above, ending with the mozzarella. Preheat oven to 350 degrees F. Cook for 1-1/2 hours or until lasagne starts to bubble. Take it out and let cool, then refrigerate overnight. The next day heat up in the oven until hot. Serves 10 to 12.

Matt Mille

As CBS Sports' top broadcaster O'Brien has brought events like the Final Four, the Winter Olympics, the Super Bowl and the World Series into America's living rooms.

March Madness Grilled Amberjack

6	4-ounce amberjack steaks (or substitute your favorite fish steak)
1/3	cup lemon juice
1/3	cup red wine vinegar
1	teaspoon sugar
1/8	teaspoon salt
1	teaspoon minced thyme
3	cloves garlic, minced
3	tablespoons cracked pepper
	Vegetable cooking spray

Place amberjack steaks in shallow dish. In a small bowl, combine lemon juice, red wine vinegar, sugar, salt, thyme and garlic. Stir well. Pour mixture over fish, turning the fish to coat both sides. Cover and marinate in the refrigerator for 30 minutes, turning occasionally. Place fish on a plate. Sprinkle pepper evenly over both sides of the fish, pressing the pepper into the fish. Spray grill with cooking spray. Place fish on grill over medium coals for 4 to 6 minutes per side. Serves 6.

Pat O'Brien

Lotta Spicy Pasta

6 mild Italian link sausages
2 tablespoons unsalted butter
1 medium onion, chopped
1-1/2 teaspoons red pepper flakes
2 1-pound cans whole Italian plum
  tomatoes, undrained
1 cup vodka
1 cup heavy cream
1 tablespoon tomato paste
1 pound penne pasta
1 cup grated Parmesan cheese
  Fresh oregano, minced, to taste

Bring enough water to cover sausages to a boil in a large pot. Add sausages and cook for 10 minutes, then remove from heat and let cool. In a saute pan, cook the onions, butter and red pepper flakes until onion is golden. Add tomatoes and simmer for one hour. Add the sausage and vodka and simmer until heated through. Turn the heat on high and add the cream and tomato paste but do not boil. Stir well. While sauce is simmering, cook pasta according to package directions, drain and place in bowl. Toss gently with sauce. Sprinkle on Parmesan cheese and oregano. Serves 6.

Theismann

Shot-Gun Sauted Chicken with Tomato & Mozzarella

4	boneless chicken breasts
4	tablespoons olive oil
2	tablespoons chopped shallot
4	ounces shiitake mushrooms and regular mushrooms combined
1	tablespoon minced garlic
1	cup chicken stock
1	tablespoon chopped fresh basil
	Salt and pepper to taste
1/2	cup madeira wine
1/4	cup heavy cream
4	slices plum tomato
4	slices mozzarella
	Pinch cumin
1	tablespoon freshly chopped parsley
2	tablespoons grated Parmesan

on
ime
with
ver

ew
p lead
o a
r the
s in
ll. He
cted
vl.
L

ll.

Saute the olive oil with the shallots, mushrooms, garlic and chicken breast. Add the chicken stock and add the fresh basil and salt and pepper to taste. Bring to a simmer and add the madeira and cream, cooking the chicken till almost done. Transfer the chicken breasts to a sizzle plate or baking pan and spoon the pan juices, herbs and vegetables on top of the chicken. Top with the plum tomato and mozzarella. Sprinkle a pinch of cumin, chopped parsley and Parmesan on top of chicken breast and bake under the broiler until the cheese melts. Serves 4.

Recipe Index

Athlete Index

Golf

Racing

Olympics

Soccer

Sportscasters

Thank you for purchasing an All Star Feast. The following three organizations will be recieving major contributions from sales of this book.

The Buoniconti Fund to Cure Paralysis

When Marc Buoniconti was injured in 1985, he and his family refused to let go of hope. His father, former All-Pro linebacker Nick Buoniconti, helped found the Miami Project toCure Paralysis, which has since become the world's premier spinal cord injury research center. With over 90 doctors, scientists and clinicians affiliated with the University of MiamiSchool of Medicine, the Miami Project has made unparalleled and spectacular findings inits efforts to find a cure. Indeed, it has generated hope for millions of people paralyzed by spinal cord injury.

Committed to finding a cure and to seeing millions worldwide walk again, the Buoniconti family and the Miami Project established the Buoniconti Fund to Cure Paralysis, a non-profit organization devoted to assisting the Miami Project achieve it national and international goals by generating high levels of awareness. The Fund's Board, comprised of many prominent Americans, will ensure that the messages of both the Buoniconti Fund and the Miami Project are seen clearly and positively by an ever-increasing audience.

With Chapters in cities throughout the country, the Buoniconti Fund serves as the national fundraising arm of the Miami Project. Together, the Miami Project and the Buoniconti Fund are working toward the day when scientists will be able to cure spinal cord injuries, and turn hope into reality.

If you would like more information about our efforts, upcoming fundraising events or to join a chapter, please contact us at:

The Buoniconti Fund to Cure Paralysis
65 West 55th Street
Suite 8E
New York, NY 10019
1-800-STANDUP

The Women's Sports Foundation
Join Our Team!

Does your daughter play sports?
Does your daughter have the same opportunities to play as your son?
Does your daughter's sports results make the morning paper or the evening news?
Does your community rally around girls sports achievements?

If you can answer no to any of these questions, this is a call to action. Take action so that your daughter can gain the same benefits from sports participation as your son. Call the Women's Sports Foundation at 1-800-227-3988 to see what you can do to make a difference. The Foundation is a national nonprofit, member-based organization dedicated to increasing opportunities for girls and women in sports and fitness through education, advocacy, recognition and grants.

Continued →

Established in 1974 by Billie Jean King, its founder; Donna de Varona, a founding member and its first president; and many other champion female athletes, the Foundation seeks to create an educated public that encourages female participation and supports gender equality in sport.

Remember when more girls play, everybody wins!

Special Olympics International

Hailed by the Chronicle of Philanthropy as the nation's most credible charity, Special Olympics provides year-round sports training and athletic competition for children and adults with mental retardation in the belief that people with mental retardation can, with proper instruction and encouragement, learn, enjoy and benefit from participation in individual and team sports. Special Olympics works to give all persons with mental retardation the chance to become useful and productive citizens who are accepted and respected in their communities. Founded by Eunice Kennedy Shriver and established by the Joseph P. Kennedy Jr. Foundation, Special Olympics strives to help people with mental retardation become physically fit and grow mentally, socially, and personally.

The international organization, with Programs in every state and more than 143 countries, began in 1968 with the first International Special Olympics Games held at Chicago's Soldier Field. Today, more than 140,000 coaches and 500,000 volunteers work with 1.2 million Special Olympics athletes in 23 official Olympic-type sports in over 15,000 games, meets and tournaments held worldwide each year.

Special Olympics organizes many programs designed to improve the lives of those with mental retardation. The Unified Sports, program brings people without mental retardation together on the same team with people with mental retardation of comparable age and athletic ability. This program fosters the integration of people with mental retardation into school and community sports programs. Special Olympics created the Motor Activities Training Program, emphasizing participation rather than competition, for athletes with severe handicaps. These programs, and others, are part of Special Olympics International's commitment to offer sports training to all individuals with mental retardation.

Special Olympics activities depend on support from volunteers and communities. For more information about how to get involved as a Special Olympics athlete, coach, official, or in another capacity, please contact your local Special Olympics Program or write to:

Special Olympics International
1325 G St. NW, Suite 500
Washington, D.C. 20005
Internet: http://www.specialolympics.org

Photo Credits

Front Cover Athletes

Gretzky, Wayne . . . . Photo Rick Stewart/AllSport
Joyner-Kersee, Jackie . . . Photo Gray Mortimore/AllSport
McPeak, Holly . . . . Photo Al Tielemans/Sports Illustrated
O'Neal, Shaquille . . . . Photo Elsa Hasch/AllSport
Ripken, Cal . . . . Photo Doug Pensinger/AllSport
Sampras, Pete . . . . Photo Al Bello/AllSport
Smith, Emmitt . . . . Photo Jamie Squire/AllSport

Back Cover Athletes

Agassi, Andre . . . . Photo Loren Haynes/
Loren Haynes Photography
Favre, Brett . . . . Photo Brian Bahr/AllSport
Holyfield, Evander . . Photo John Iacono/Sports Illustrated
Johnson, Michael . . . . Photo Simone Bruty/AllSport
Seles, Monica . . . . Photo Clive Brunskill/AllSport
Street, Picabo . . . . Photo Simon Bruty/AllSport
Strug, Kerri . . . . Photo Doug Pensinger/AllSport

Table of Contents . . . . Photo Barry Hart
Kitchen of Bernie Cyrus, Louisiana Music Commissioner

Baseball

Karros, Eric . . . . Photo V.J. Lovero
Piazza, Mike . . . . Photo V.J. Lovero
Ripken, Cal . . . . Photo Walter Iooss

Boxing

Holyfield, Evander . . . . Photo Michael Weaver

Football

Esiason, Boomer. . . . . Photo Rick Stewart/AllSport
Favre, Brett. . . . . Photo Walter Iooss, Jr.
. . . . Photo Rich Frishman
Montana, Joe . . . . Photo Walter Iooss
Peete, Rodney . . . . Photo Jed Jacobsohn/AllSport
Smith, Emmitt . . . . Photo Robert Beck

Golf

Floyd, Raymond . . . . Photo J.D. Cuban/AllSport
Lopez, Nancy . . . . Photo Ken Levine
Sorenstam, Annika . . . . Photo Robert Beck

Hockey

Gretzky, Wayne . . . . Photo Walter Iooss
Robitaille, Luc. . . . . Photo Crop Whitehall

Olympic

Blair, Bonnie . . . . Photo Rick Stewart/AllSport
Boitano, Brian . . . . Photo David Cannon/AllSport
Joyner-Kersee, Jackie. . . . Photo Gray Mortimore/AllSport
Lewis, Carl. . . . . Photo Mike Powell/AllSport
Miller, Shannon . . . . Photo Cary Garrison
Tomba, Alberto . . . . Photo Armando Rotoletti
Yamaguchi, Kristy . . . . Photo Wyatt Counts
Van Dyken, Amy. . . . . Photo Annie Leibovitz

Racing

Andretti, Mario . . . . Photo Dan R. Boyd/AllSport
Andretti, Michael. . . . . Photo Dan R. Boyd/AllSport
Fittipaldi, Christian . . . . Photo Dan R. Boyd/AllSport
Fittipaldi, Emerson. . . . . Photo David Taylor/AllSport
Vasser, Jimmy. . . . . Photo Denny Young/IMG

Sportscasters

Brown, James . . . . Photo Aaron Rapoport/
Fox Broadcasting Company
Costas, Bob . . . . Photo NBC Broadcasting Company
Enberg, Dick. . . . . Photo Kimberly Butler/
NBC Broadcasting Company
Gifford, Frank. . . . . Photo Gary Bernstein.
Long, Howie . . . . Photo Fox Broadcasing Company
Millen, Matt. . . . . Photo George Feder

Tennis

Agassi, Andre . . . . Photo John Russell
Evert, Chris . . . . Photo Jonathon Exley
Jensen, Luke . . . . Photo Chris Cole/AllSport
Jensen, Murphy . . . . Photo Chris Cole/AllSport
Navratilova, Martina . . . . Photo Trevor Jones/AllSport
Sampras, Pete . . . . Photo Jeff Schwartz
Seles, Monica . . . . Photo Michael Baz

Author photo of Wendy Diamond . . . Photo Mychal Watts

Sporting Equipment in Wendy Diamond's author
photo courtesy of **Franklin** SPORTS

All backgrounds were contributed by
Digital Stock, Metatools and Photodisc.

All trading cards were contributed by
Fleer/Sky Box International.

Acknowledgements

Where do I start ????? First, I am apologizing for anyone I missed, as if you didn't call me the day I was writing this I could easily and of course accidentally forgotten! First, my parents, for bringing me on to this earth to do such great fun things! Sisters, Marcy, Hilary, Tina especially Renay and Cynthia who dealt with this project more than anyone should have had to! Aunt Dianne two down! The Sports Consultants: Maury Gostfrand, J.B. Morris, Craig Stanton and Bob Benjamin. The committee Catherine Williams and Elizabeth Parella. Everyone at Blue Marble! Marquee -Mike Levine and Michael George. Email king, Allen Tuller. Nick Pritzker for my first athlete, Michael Jordan! Sal Schiliro and Ann Marie DeNapoli at Street, Smith's & Diamond! Karin Arnold, Jeff Schwartz, Denny Young and everyone at IMG! Steve Mayer-TWI, Phil Ippolito, John Urban-MSG, Rich Russo and JL Media. Melanie Young, SOI-Peter Wheeler, Christina Burns and Mary Ruppe, the BF-Abbe Ruttenberg, Paul Costiglio, Nick Buoniconti, WSF-Nirva, Rachel, Donna and Tuti. The Chicago Connections, Dimitri Alexander and Linda Spitz. Brad Hunt and everyone at Gold Medal Mgmt. Ted Kelly, Frank Murphy @ CBS Radio, the recipe testers : Christy Wood, Susan Ross, Tomm Taylor, Charlie Hecht, Kathy Araskog, Joanna Ifrah, Craig Minassian, Chris Pepe @ MLS, Marissa Mencher, Mitchell Simmons, Jodi Gottlieb. Elena Zazanis, Mark Calabrese and all the people who had to eat! Marvin Girouard-Mr. Pier 1, Constance Schwartz & Dave Houghton @NFL Properties, Brad Schlachter@ MLB, Brad Hunt and all at Gold Medal Mgmt, KICK 10-Mark Stein, Michael Terry 4 Emmitt, Neal Tiles @ Fox Sports, Mark Dorian, Peter Orlowsky-AllSport, Peter Stern, SI-Matt Ginella, ISI- Jamey it's over!, Patricia Jensen, Gabe Harris-Advantage Intl, Richie Rountree, Phil Pfeffer, Lynn Swann, Leo Hart, Jamie Diamond, Michael and the Bader Group, Rita Wolfson, David Bloom, Jonathon Lynne, Tanya Moby Dick, Sandra Griffin, Larry Friedman, Danny Hayes, CEO-Lisa Rogen, Arthur Sando, Roger Dreyer, Lisa Abdula, Caryl Chinn, Joel Karlik, Lee Stern-B&N, Mark Grand, Gino Giorgini III, and Bill Stutts, Tom Freet, Sue Sylvester, Beth Slanina and Sonia Rivera-Hooey at Beckley! The All Star Chefs- Randy Pietro-Mickey Mantles, John Gray-Grand Havana Room, and the connoisseur of sports and food, Bert Padell! This list could go on and on and on…

National Coalition for the Homeless, New York Coalition for the Homeless, Coalition on Homelessness-San Francisco and Empty the Shelters for bringing me such fulfillment in my life with the success of A Musical Feast.

Everyone at the Buoniconti Fund to Cure Paralysis, Special Olympics International, and Women's Sports Foundation for their support and dedication to their causes!

I know there are many people I did not mention but here to sum it up- Thanks to everyone-every athlete and athlete's family, who took the time to contribute recipes, anecdotes and photos, every friend, lawyer, agent and manager. This project would not of been possible without the thousand or more people who have been helpful in making this book happen and to raise funds for the charities benefitting.

Thanks especially to our sponsors who made this book happen and supported this project to raise money for many less privileged. **Rajan Shah at Diet Coke**
Patty Proferes, Katie Carter and Mary Panus at 1 800 Collect
Gretchen Millspaugh, Denise Gawronski, Bill Bordegon and everyone at Fleer/SkyBox International
Kurt Graetzer at International Dairy Foods Association

What's Mike Ditka's Recipe for Savings?

Mike's Recipe

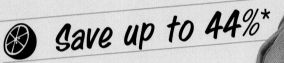 Dial 1-800-COLLECT

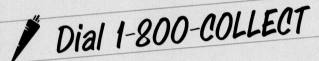 Save up to 44%*

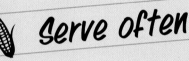 Serve often

1-800-COLLECT proudly supports the All-Star Feast which benefits:

Buoniconti Fund to Cure Paralysis, Women's Sports Foundation and Special Olympics International

1-800-COLLECT